Faith-based Diplomacy and Interfaith Dialogue

Diplomacy and Foreign Policy

Volumes published in this Brill Research Perspective are listed at *brill.com/rpdf*

Faith-based Diplomacy and Interfaith Dialogue

By

Scott Blakemore

BRILL

LEIDEN | BOSTON

This paperback book edition is simultaneously published as issue 3.2 (2018), in *Diplomacy and Foreign Policy*, DOI:10.1163/24056006-12340010.

Library of Congress Control Number: 2019941637

Typeface for the Latin, Greek, and Cyrillic scripts: "Brill". See and download: brill.com/brill-typeface.

ISBN 978-90-04-40892-0 (paperback)
ISBN 978-90-04-40895-1 (e-book)

This book is printed on acid-free paper and produced in a sustainable manner.

Contents

Faith-based Diplomacy and Interfaith Dialogue

Scott Blakemore
Bond University
sblakemo@bond.edu.au

Abstract

Scholars are seeking to identify how to integrate faith into diplomacy constructively. Proponents of faith-based diplomacy recognise that incorporating faith into peacemaking activities assists in alleviating identity-based conflict and religiously motivated violence in the contemporary international system. A promising strategy within the scope of faith-based diplomacy is interfaith dialogue. The study and practice of interfaith dialogue have been reinvigorated since the advent of 9/11, and yet the link between interfaith dialogue and diplomacy remains underdeveloped. The cases of Indonesia and the United States show that states can effectively use interfaith dialogue to achieve policy objectives, and yet some policies are detrimental to achieving goals. Faith-based diplomacy and interfaith dialogue can be innovative diplomatic perspectives useful in addressing contemporary global issues.

Keywords

interfaith – faith-based – dialogue – diplomacy

Supplementary materials including a slide presentation and a video prepared by the author can be accessed at https://brill.figshare.com/s/6ea855cd48def174d07a

1 Introduction

Faith in diplomacy can be understood in many ways. To some, this may be understood as confidence in the diplomatic system, enhanced by generating faith in the institutions and mechanisms of diplomacy. To do this, scholars and practitioners are required to fully appreciate the current trends, dynamics and challenges evident in the international environment. Another way to understand faith in diplomacy is by considering the place of faith and religious

 | DOI:10.1163/9789004408951_002

considerations in diplomatic practice. Indeed, the community of faith would require greater participation, understanding and integration into diplomatic theory and practice to see their faith in diplomacy strengthened. After the 9/11 attacks, the War on Terror and the rise of extremist groups around the world, religion has been brought back into the sight of observers. While many see the obvious connection that has been evident through the history of religion as a motivator of violence, some are now renewing the potential of religion as a tool for peace. Within the scope of Diplomacy Studies in particular, the role of religion is being re-examined. Not only has religion been a central element of the human experience, but it has also featured heavily in the development of the international system.[1] Littered through history are examples of where religion has been directly linked with great conflict and conquests, including the Crusades or even the Thirty Years' War, which led to the development of international relations as it is known today. Even in the contemporary international environment, transnational conflict, mass media and the rhetoric of world leaders have fuelled the debate surrounding the involvement of religion in politics and society. As an example, the migrant crisis of religious minorities around the world has been presented in a way to manipulate public opinions concerning security, while terrorist attacks that claim religious legitimacy continue to challenge the positive place of religion in society.[2] Beyond this common recognition of religion's link to conflict, tools for religion's inclusion in peacemaking are being developed. Religious peacemakers have constructed a variety of approaches to incorporate religious norms, values, texts and ideas into peacemaking processes. Al Qurtuby notes that some have used religious concepts of forgiveness to enhance reconciliation processes, while others highlight compassion, peace and humanity as underpinning values to make religious peacemaking more effective.[3] Incorporating these values, and the institutions and structures of religion, into diplomacy is an opportunity that warrants the critical attention of the theorists and practitioners of diplomacy.

The purpose of this paper is to present two areas of study which seek to positively integrate religion into the diplomatic mechanisms of the international system. The first is faith-based diplomacy. The theoretical framework of faith-based diplomacy will be discussed to highlight how this framework can contribute to the effective practices of diplomacy. The purpose of the analysis of faith-based diplomacy is to provide scholars and practitioners with a

1 Daniel Philpott, "The Religious Roots of Modern International Relations," *World Politics* 52, no. 2 (2000).

2 Andrew Orton, "Interfaith Dialogue: Seven Key Questions for Theory, Policy and Practice," *Religion, State & Society* 44, no. 4 (2016): 350.

3 Sumanto Al Qurtuby, "Peacebuilding in Indonesia: Christian–Muslim Alliances in Ambon Island," *Islam and Christian–Muslim Relations* 24, no. 3 (2013): 362.

renewed perspective of faith in diplomacy with practical concepts that can be applied to future study and strategy. In simple terms, Douglas Johnston defines faith-based diplomacy in two ways. He argues that, "at the macro level, it simply means incorporating religious considerations into the practice of international politics. At the micro level, it means actually making religion part of the solution in some of today's intractable, identity-based conflicts that escape the grasp of traditional diplomacy."[4] Typically states do not have the resources or frameworks to effectively understand religion or manage religious challenges. To rectify this, faith-based diplomacy seeks to provide decisionmakers with the tools to clarify religious issues and to manage faith-based conflict.

The second area of study examined in this paper is interfaith dialogue. While this concept has been investigated thoroughly in comparative theology and religious studies, the convergent aspects of this concept and diplomacy are underdeveloped. The United States Institute of Peace defines interfaith dialogue, at its simplest form, as a way of bringing together people of different faiths to engage in conversation to develop mutual understanding between participants.[5] Within this paper it is argued that interfaith dialogue can be a valuable tool to the diplomatic community as it can function as an operationalised form of faith-based diplomacy. By highlighting methods, opportunities and limitations revealed in the literature of interfaith dialogue, this paper presents ways in which interfaith dialogue can be incorporated as an effective tool within the scope of diplomacy in the future. The evaluation of faith-based diplomacy and interfaith dialogue will underpin the two-part premise of this paper. First, that faith-based diplomacy is an important perspective in contemporary Diplomacy Studies worthy of further development, and second, that interfaith dialogue is an opportune framework to bring into the practice of faith-based diplomacy.

To support these central arguments, the methodology of this paper is set in two parts. The first part is a comprehensive literature review that consolidates the available research on faith-based diplomacy and interfaith dialogue. Key texts that develop the theoretical frameworks of faith-based diplomacy will be given critical attention to lay the foundation of scholarly analysis. The literature on interfaith dialogue will follow, drawing on scholarly journals and articles to present how interfaith dialogue is currently understood. The second part of this paper's methodology is to evaluate the way that two states

4 D. Johnston, "Faith-Based Diplomacy: Bridging the Religious Divide" Wheatly Papers on International Affairs https://wheatley.byu.edu/wp-content/uploads/2017/08/Douglas_Johnston_WebVersion.pdf, 2.

5 See United States Institute of Peace, "What Works? Evaluating Interfaith Dialogue Programs" (United States Institute of Peace 2004), 2.

have incorporated interfaith dialogue into policy and strategy. The first case examines Indonesia's utilisation of interfaith dialogue, while the second case focuses on the United States of America (US). Both cases detail several examples of where interfaith dialogue has been employed as a part of a conflict resolution or post-conflict rebuilding strategy. These examples have been drawn from journals, articles and relevant government policies. The cases aim to give a broad overview of how these states have incorporated interfaith dialogue into diplomatic strategy to evaluate the potential for interfaith dialogue to become a more prominent feature of the practice of faith-based diplomacy.

Extending upon the general approach taken to the methodology and structure of this paper, it is important to examine the form of analysis that will underpin the hypothesis of this study, that is, whether this paper is conducting causal or constitutive analysis to examine faith-based diplomacy and interfaith dialogue. These approaches, along with the literature on research methodology within International Relations, are argued extensively elsewhere, and it is not within the scope of this paper to contribute to that discussion. However, these approaches will be briefly defined to determine which is most appropriate in explaining the following study. Both causal and constitutive analysis describe, explain and help bring understanding to concepts.[6] In simple terms, causal theories are built to answer questions of 'why?' something occurs, and may give some description on how that takes place.[7] This type of analysis leads to hypotheses that often test dependent and independent variables to explain how the relationship between these variables causes a certain behaviour to occur.

Constitutive analysis, however, seeks to satisfy different research objectives. Centrally, constitutive theories "account for the properties of things by reference to the structures in virtue of which they exist."[8] Because structures within society are dynamic and often change, constitutive theory enables a snapshot of those processes to explain the constitution of those systems. As such, constitutive analysis is most concerned with "how something is possible and what it is" leading to arguments being evaluated "in terms of their conceptual or logical necessity, but never causally."[9] The focus then becomes not on why something comes about, but what it actually is.[10] When applying this line of

6 A. Wendt, "On Constitution and Causation in International Relations," *Rev. Int. Stud.* 24 (1998): 102, 117.

7 Ibid., 104.

8 Ibid., 105.

9 Richard Ned Lebow, "Constitutive Causality: Imagined Spaces and Political Practices," *Millennium – Journal of International Studies* 38, no. 2 (2009): 213.

10 Wendt, "On Constitution and Causation in International Relations," 105.

thinking to the study in this paper, it is clear that the purpose of this paper does not align with causal analysis. This paper is not seeking to explain why interfaith dialogue works, or why faith-based diplomacy is effective in certain cases. Instead, this paper prioritises understanding what the concepts of faith-based diplomacy and interfaith dialogue are. The analysis also considers the dynamic social factors, namely religion and identity, that inform the defining features of these concepts.

By focusing on the concept, and the structures that constitute that concept, there is some explanatory capacity in this form of analysis. The effects of the varying structures within a concept can be explained by looking at changes to its constitution.[11] This allows observers to identify how these concepts work together, and then make hypotheses on how the broader concept will behave within a certain environment. At the base level, this constitutive theory enables understanding through description.[12] While some may argue that description is a superficial form of analysis, it goes beyond noting observation as it requires theory "to unite and make sense of them," meaning that constitutive theories provide descriptions that are not causal, but still explanatory.[13] Understanding description in this way enables 'explanatory leverage' as they "capture the properties and dispositions of the systems they represent, even if they do not relate effects to independently existing causes."[14] This type of explanation is important not because it reveals "how or why a thing came about, or what it is, but by telling us how its elements are composed and organized so that it has the properties that it does."[15] Within the purview of this study, constitutive analysis of interfaith dialogue allows the concept to be explained in terms of what it is and how it is comprised. This affords an explanation of what the concept is and how it might be applied. In line with John Ruggie's preference of 'constitutive causality', this analysis "has the potential to lead us back step-by-step to 'deep' causes of political outcomes, and forward again in an ever-widening, more comprehensive search for connections and causes."[16] Thus, constitutive analysis that understands the changing relationship of components within a concept, and the way this may influence the behaviour of that concept as a whole, can result in hypotheses that can be tested empirically. As the central purposes of this paper are to highlight the perspective of faith-based diplomacy within Diplomacy Studies, and to explain the framework of interfaith dialogue as a form of faith-based diplomacy, this paper will undertake a

11 Ibid., 106.
12 Ibid., 108.
13 Ibid., 108.
14 Ibid., 111.
15 Ibid., 112.
16 Lebow, "Constitutive Causality: Imagined Spaces and Political Practices," 213-215.

constitutive perspective of analysis to explain what these concepts are, what constitutes these concepts, and how these concepts might behave within a certain environment.

The analysis of how faith interacts with diplomacy is increasingly important as the dynamics of religion are contributing to divisions and conflicts between social groups in the globalised world.[17] In fact, the influence of globalisation has seen several important developments when examining the impact of religion in society, including the spread of different religious groups across borders, the exporting of religions into new regions, the hybridisation of different religious traditions, and the increasing need for pluralism in society.[18] As these dynamics of religion enforce patterns of behaviour and relationships, the concern is that the likelihood of constructive dialogue occurring between these diverse groups becomes less likely.[19] As a result, different groups often live alongside each other, but choose not to interact meaningfully.[20] This trend, however, cannot be ignored as it can contribute to marginalisation potentially leading to violent conflict. McCormack warns that discourse "around the social dimensions of religion can no longer be considered comprehensive without taking into account the complex dynamics and implications of the interfaith encounter."[21] Hence, not only must religion be appreciated more as a factor in identity, conflicts and politics, but increasingly the interaction between religious groups must be taken more seriously by policymakers.

This attention is difficult to manage, however, as the relationship between religion and politics has long been controversial. Since the advent of Westphalian Peace, religion has been separated from the political authority of the state and made into a domestic affair. The 'box and tame' approach, as Sharp calls it, saw religion relegated even further from political structures and made into a solely personal experience.[22] This, along with modernisation and scientific discovery, led certain observers to believe that religion would eventually lose its influence in society as a result of a clear separation between church

17 Orton, "Interfaith Dialogue: Seven Key Questions for Theory, Policy and Practice," 349-350.

18 See Peter Beyer and Lori G. Beaman, *Religion, Globalization and Culture* (Leiden, Boston: Brill, 2007). Also see José Casanova, "Religion, the New Millennium, and Globalization," *Sociology of Religion* 62, no. 4 (2001).

19 Orton, "Interfaith Dialogue: Seven Key Questions for Theory, Policy and Practice," 349-50.

20 Ibid., 350. This concept is in line with Cantle's notion of 'parallel lives', see Ted Cantle, "Parallel Lives," *Index on Censorship* 35, no. 2 (2006).

21 Mark M. McCormack, "Interfaith Relations in the United States: Toward a Multilevel Community Psychology Approach," *Journal of Community & Applied Social Psychology* 23, no. 3 (2013): 171.

22 See Paul Sharp, "Crazy Religion Diplomacy," in *Diplomatic Theory of International Relations* (United Kingdom: Cambridge University Press, 2009).

and state, commonly referred to as the secularisation thesis. Over time, however, this thesis has been challenged. Critics of the thesis contest the nature of secularisation and how secularisation works in a variety of contexts.[23] This is exemplified by the fact that certain states and religions place religion on different levels of importance and incorporate religion into their political structures in various ways. Ultimately, the fundamental premise of the secularisation thesis has not withstood the events of history. Indeed, even strong proponents of the thesis recognise that the world today is "as furiously religious as it ever was, and in some places more so than ever" rendering the central claim of secularisation as flawed.[24] Even within the scope of secularisation, however, political science and psychology recognise the importance of religion as a component of culture and identity, and by extension in ethnopolitical and identity-based conflicts.[25] While progress has been made in recognising the part religion can play in resolving identity-based conflicts, its role can often be either neglected or overemphasised when considering its place in responding to intractable conflicts.[26] This is due to the continued challenge of incorporating religion effectively into policy and decision-making as state structures are still reticent to engage with religious considerations. In the modern context, the religious-secular distinctions in international politics has been challenging, but there are cases where religion has been able to find a place within governance structures.[27] With the adherents to religious traditions increasing around the globe, and religion still being a major factor in much of the conflicts across the world today, the traditional concept of secularisation does not adequately explain the current international system. Hence, some scholars suggest that the international system is moving into a postsecular era.

The various religious challenges impacting the current international system has brought the emergence of what some call 'postsecular governance'.[28] Religious individuals and groups have long been seeking to play a positive part in contributing to political processes while still playing an active role in the community.[29] As a result, structures of governance have adjusted to

23 Orton, "Interfaith Dialogue: Seven Key Questions for Theory, Policy and Practice," 350.

24 Luke Bretherton, "A Postsecular Politics? Inter-Faith Relations as a Civic Practice," *Journal of the American Academy of Religion* 79, no. 2 (2011): 112.

25 Reina C. Neufeldt, "Interfaith Dialogue: Assessing Theories of Change," *Peace & Change* 36, no. 3 (2011): 358.

26 Mohammed Abu-Nimer, "Religious Leaders in the Israeli-Palestinian Conflict: From Violent Incitement to Nonviolence Resistance," ibid., no. 4, 556.

27 See Trevor Stack et al., *Religion as a Category of Governance and Sovereignty* (Leiden, Netherlands and Boston, Massachusetts: Brill, 2015).

28 Orton, "Interfaith Dialogue: Seven Key Questions for Theory, Policy and Practice," 351.

29 Ibid., 351.

incorporate religious contributions at various levels. This has developed a complex network of relationships which, while recognising a place for religion, is limited by friction between actors that needs to be navigated. Bretherton defines the postsecularist period as one where, "multiple modernities, each with their respective relationship to religious belief and practice, are overlapping and interacting within the same shared, predominantly urban spaces" which suggests that elite groups within the state must be more mindful of the public presence of religion.[30] If indeed the international system is shifting to postsecularism, this allows scholars and practitioners to engage meaningfully with religion without the historical reticence generally felt toward the topic. This postsecular environment is fertile ground to investigate the positive role religion can have in the international system, namely with a renewed perspective of the potentialities in diplomacy. Along with this, intercultural and interfaith dialogue has been put forward as a mechanism for potentially resolving problems that arise in the current global environment.[31] While this form of governance appears quite complex, the conceptualisation of hybrid actors, actors that represent both the state and religion, can influence state policy as well as religious factors which extend beyond traditional state structures.[32] As states, diplomats, and scholars continue to investigate the possibilities of a postsecular space, religion can be understood with more clarity and utilised more effectively to engage in the challenges of the 21st century.

A watershed moment in the 21st century which has undeniably changed the course of international relations was the attacks on September 11, 2001. This event brought religion back into the spotlight of analysis for those in international relations, and the consequences of this event are still being felt. Mandour suggests that, since these attacks, interest in the process of interfaith dialogue has significantly increased as "an essential tool for bridging the ideological divide in modern societies, especially those with multiple identities and religious pluralism, deeply shaped by globalization."[33] The consequences of 9/11, and the implications of the events that followed highlighted that the practitioners working in the field were unprepared and untrained for the cross-religious dialogues that became necessary.[34]

30 Bretherton, "A Postsecular Politics? Inter-Faith Relations as a Civic Practice," 354.

31 Orton, "Interfaith Dialogue: Seven Key Questions for Theory, Policy and Practice," 351.

32 See Katharina McLarren and Bernhard Stahl, "'Hybrid Actors' – Religion and the Shift Towards a World Society" in *ECPR General Conference* (Montreal 2015).

33 Tayseir Mandour, "Islam and Religious Freedom: Role of Interfaith Dialogue in Promoting Global Peace," *Brigham Young University Law Review* 2010, no. 3 (2010): 886.

34 Julie Clague, "Political Theology Ten Years after 9/11," *Political Theology* 12, no. 5 (2011): 466.

9/11, and the American response to the event,[35] saw religion and conflict thrusted into international peacemaking concerns, namely in the Middle East. Militant terrorist groups such as the so-called 'Islamic State,' have destabilised regions and impacted the public perceptions of religion. Populist trends around the world have heightened the fear of marginalisation and potential for conflict, if not at the very least impacting social cohesion in many parts of the world. Magonet notes that the 'War on Terror' incited ideological divisions reminiscent of Huntington's Clash of Civilizations assumptions, along with the revelation of Western ignorance of Islam resulting in increasing levels of Islamophobia.[36] These issues suggest a more productive integration of religious principles in peacemaking activities, seeing that interfaith dialogue provides the opportunity to resist "the fundamentalist currents in the world religions" and promote solidarity between religious groups as a counter to power imbalances projected elsewhere on the global stage.[37] All of these challenges have revealed a need to engage in dialogue between religious groups and effectively utilise diplomatic mechanisms to better manage religious issues. The misunderstandings and tension between people of different religious traditions highlight interfaith dialogue as a method of peacebuilding with various actors working to understand how to create spaces for successful engagement, and creative techniques to go beyond traditional mechanisms.[38]

The roots of interfaith dialogue, however, run much deeper than as a reactionary policy following 9/11 with encounters between religions being common throughout history. In fact, even religious texts document engagements between religious groups. However, when considering the events that have most contributed to the contemporary landscape regarding religion and diplomacy, a major turning point in the growth of interfaith dialogue comes from Nostra Aetate – an event which will be discussed in much more detail later in this paper. This document was released by the Roman Catholic Church in 1965 and opened the institution to interfaith dialogue. This document paid particular attention to the relationship with Judaism, and thus many formal dialogues between members of the Catholic and Jewish community began

35 See Daniel Philpott, "The Challenge of September 11 to Secularism in International Relations," *World Politics* 55, no. 1 (2002).

36 Jonathan Magonet, "The Growth of Interfaith Dialogue," *European Judaism* 48, no. 2 (2015): 41.

37 Gregory Baum, "Interreligious Dialogue Includes Listening to Secular Voices," *Toronto Journal of Theology* 32, no. 2 (2016): 363.

38 Roberta R. King, "Music, Peacebuilding, and Interfaith Dialogue: Transformative Bridges in Muslim–Christian Relations," *International Bulletin of Mission Research* 40, no. 3 (2016): 203-204.

to form.[39] Beyond this starting point, however, Nostra Aetate paved the way for other major religions to begin communicating, which has been a healthy platform to work from in developing peace processes. These events demonstrate that there are frames and mechanisms that have been tested throughout time to engage with the impact of religion on the international system. However, the challenges of the 21st century have shown that these mechanisms must be re-evaluated to see diplomatic outcomes improved.

1.1 *Definitions and Key Terms*

Before investigating the frameworks and methods of integrating faith in diplomatic practice, it is important to recognise that throughout scholarship religion and its related concepts have deeply contested meanings. When considering a topic so central to identity, it is imperative to be as precise with meanings as possible. The literature surrounding the definition of faith, religion and spirituality is substantial and the scope of this paper does not allow for a detailed discussion on the nuances of these terms.[40] However, for the purposes of this paper, simple definitions of religion, faith and dialogue will be provided to clarify what is meant by these terms throughout, but they are by no means reflective of the significant body of literature on the topic.

When defining religion, Neufeldt notes that there are four broad elements that inform religion being, theological beliefs and values, religious practices, behavioural norms, and a confessional community.[41] These components then influence culture, society and an individual's behaviour, identity and thought.[42] Swidler agrees, suggesting that religion contains the four 'C's', being creed, code, cult and community-structure.[43] This conceptualisation of religion recognises the cognitive aspect of religion, the way that behaviour is informed by religion, the public and private activities related to the believer, and also the relationships that form between believers which informs a common identity.[44] With these characteristics embedded within the idea of religion, Johnston defines religion as "an institutional framework within which specific theological doctrines and practices are advocated and pursued, usually among a

39 Magonet, "The Growth of Interfaith Dialogue," 38-9.

40 For a discussion on the contested nature of these concepts, see Brian J. Zinnbauer et al., "Religion and Spirituality: Unfuzzying the Fuzzy," *Journal for the Scientific Study of Religion* 36, no. 4 (1997).

41 Neufeldt, "Interfaith Dialogue: Assessing Theories of Change," 346.

42 Ibid., 346.

43 Leonard Swidler, "Sorting out Meanings: 'Religion,' 'Spiritual,' 'Interreligious,' 'Interfaith,' Etc.," *Journal of Ecumenical Studies* 49, no. 3 (2014).

44 Ibid., 374.

community of like-minded believers."[45] The definition of religion generally returns to how theological beliefs and practices are institutionalised, which often translates to religion being understood as an ordering mechanism for global society.[46] The way in which religion informs identity has long been of interest to scholars, however, observers are now recognising that religious identity is a much more dynamic process that is being interpreted and reconstructed in contemporary society.[47] Sociologists have used the word 'hybrid' and 'bricolage' to emphasise that there are positive aspects of the mixing of various religious perspectives.[48] Both of these terms, in Suomala's perspective, "emphasise mixture and point to the fluid and multitextured nature of religious identity" which further highlights the need for understanding how best to navigate between faiths.[49]

The term faith is closely associated with that of religion, but there are subtle differences to these ideas which are important in this topic. Defining faith with similar clarity is difficult in the context of International Relations. Faith often "transcends the normal parameters of organised religions" as it is a "less bounded and, at times, more far-reaching scope of human involvement."[50] Thus, the term faith seeks to go beyond the institutional and behavioural elements of religion. Faith focuses the way a person, or a collective group of people, see the world and their place within it, how humanity derives meaning and purpose, and how humanity is connected to the sacred.[51] The reason that the term faith is favoured over the term religion in the discussion of theory in this paper is that it is a broader concept that takes into account not only the structures of religion, but the personal, identity-based elements of the individual. Faith is a broader conception that allows for more flexibility in theoretical analysis and also suggests various degrees of religious involvement. Throughout this paper, both religion and faith will be used, but religion will suggest the institutional manifestation of beliefs, and faith will refer to the identity-based nature of religion.

---

45 Douglas Johnston, "Introduction: Beyond Power Politics," in *Religion, the Missing Dimension of Statecraft*, ed. Douglas Johnston and Cynthia Sampson (New York: Oxford University Press, 1994), 4.

46 For more on this notion of ordering, see Andrew Phillips, *War, Religion and Empire: The Transformation of International Orders* (Cambridge: Cambridge University Press, 2011).

47 Karla Suomala, "Complex Religious Identity in the Context of Interfaith Dialogue," *Cross Currents* 62, no. 3 (2012): 364.

48 Ibid., 364.

49 Ibid., 364.

50 Johnston, "Introduction: Beyond Power Politics," 4.

51 J. Mark Lazenby, "On "Spirituality," "Religion," and "Religions": A Concept Analysis," *Palliative and Supportive Care* 8, no. 4 (2010): 469-470.

It is on this basis of the contemporary trends of globalisation and interactivity between groups the interfaith dialogue has been built. Swidler offers a detailed definition of dialogue which is important to consider when applying to the context of dialogue between groups. Swidler's definition states that:

> The term 'dialogue' has long been part of the English language, but in recent decades it has taken on a greatly deepened meaning, especially in the area of religion. It comes originally from two Greek words, dia, "across," "together," and logos, "thinking," as in "logic," and all the words ending in "logy," meaning systematic thinking about something ... Secondarily, it means the expression of our thinking, "words." Thus, literally "dai-logue" means "thinking and speaking together.[52]

Swidler continues to build on this definition of dialogue by again stressing the deeper aspects of dialogue which comes back to the focus on learning together.[53] The concept of dialogue needs to be carefully considered when translating the word in different languages. Ali-Dib notes the challenge of using dialogue in Syria as the translation used for dialogue promoted conversion and immediately hindered progress between groups.[54] Words like 'coexistence' and 'friendship' were suggested instead to curb the immediate reticence in terminology.[55] A more detailed exploration of the meaning and implications of interfaith dialogue will be undertaken later in the paper, but for the purposes of this introduction, the term dialogue suggests Swidler's explanation of thinking and speaking together.

The discussion of these definitions, while brief, demonstrates the complexity of these concepts. When translated into the scope of international relations, or diplomacy more specifically, this complexity must be appreciated. As the dynamics of religion and faith become a more pressing concern in diplomatic and political considerations, this paper seeks to clarify what scholarly and practical frameworks are presently available for faith-based diplomacy and interfaith dialogue. These frameworks offer a new perspective on the mechanisms of diplomacy which may assist in resolving identity-based conflict, enhancing post-conflict peacebuilding, supporting reconciliation, and promoting communal harmony. The potential of these frameworks

52 Swidler, "Sorting out Meanings: 'Religion,' 'Spiritual,' 'Interreligious,' 'Interfaith,' Etc.," 376.

53 "Deeper Meanings of Dialogue Today," *Journal of Ecumenical Studies* 48, no. 2 (2013): 143.

54 Edith Szanto Ali-Dib, "Inter-Religious Dialogue in Syria: Politics, Ethics and Miscommunication," *Political Theology* 9, no. 1 (2008): 94.

55 Ibid., 94.

re-affirm that faith-based diplomacy is an important perspective in contemporary Diplomacy Studies which can be advanced by incorporating interfaith dialogue into its practice.

2 Faith-based Diplomacy

2.1 *Context and History of Faith-based Diplomacy*

Religion has long been recognised a powerful force within the community and while some may have suggested that religion would fade away in terms of global influence as society pursued modernity, the place and influence of religion is still very much a factor in the current global environment. Patterson suggests five reasons as to why religion has experienced a resurgence in global attention which are pertinent to the construction of policy and international relations. First, individual religiosity is increasing over the world. Second, individual and group expressions of religion in public is becoming more important in political discourse. Third, the role of the state in providing services and being the sole source of legitimate authority and authenticity is being challenged. Fourth, the actors, ideas and identities of religion are increasingly transnational. And fifth, what is often considered a rational or material interest, whether individually or collectively, can be transcended by religious motivations.[56] These are reasons as to why religion has become an important consideration of policy-makers, not to mention the way in which nature of conflict has transformed in the international system to give more weight to the power of religion. However, due to the historical relationship between church and state, and the structures that separate church and state, policymakers are reticent to engage with religion and often disregard the role of "religion, religious institutions, and religious motivations in explaining politics and conflict."[57]

The nature of conflict in the 21st century has shifted as the majority of conflicts are now intractable, identity-based conflicts in which the structures and mechanisms of diplomacy are not able to manage the ethnic, tribal and religious manifestations of violence.[58] Johnston suggests that religious conflicts have intensified due to economic globalisation confronting traditional

56 Cited in Lee Marsden, "Faith-Based Diplomacy: Conservative Evangelicals and the United States Military," *Politics and Religion* 7, no. 3 (2014): 477.

57 Edward Luttwak, "The Missing Dimension," in *Religion, the Missing Dimension of Statecraft*, ed. Douglas & Sampson Johnston, Cynthia (New York: Oxford University Press, 1994), 9.

58 Douglas M. Johnston, "An Asymmetric Counter to the Asymmetric Threat," *American Foreign Policy Interests* 35, no. 1 (2013): 10.

religious values, world populations being fragmented due to rapid technological change, the economic divide between groups worsening, and secular governments not being able to adequately satisfy the expectations of their populations.[59] While religious and cultural differences have been clearly identified in the literature as a motivating force in conflicts, the paradigm shift taking place in scholarship is based on recognising that the spiritual depths of faith and religion house positive assets that can be utilised in the diplomatic process to de-escalate tension and mitigate violent conflict.[60] This has seen a renewed focus on the methods and processes of conflict resolution. The West has been unable to manage religious differences through the mechanisms of conflict resolution, with the rational-actor framework and traditional methods of diplomacy not being able to fully recognise the role of nonstate actors and communal reconciliation, for example.[61] The avenues by which religious actors can engage in conflict is becoming a more pertinent conversation, along with the way in which religious values can support resolution processes.[62] Due to the pressure placed on the institution of diplomacy and the conflict resolution field more broadly, religion has had to be given a more meaningful place in the practice and theory of diplomacy, hence the emergence of faith-based diplomacy as a field of study.

The theory of faith-based diplomacy emerged in 1994,[63] yet its practice has been evident in diplomacy through history. Diplomacy between faith groups is not a new phenomenon, but it is a difficult process.[64] However, the frameworks have only recently been introduced and evaluated in scholarship. While perhaps a simple link, former Secretary of State Madeleine Albright explains that if the central purpose of diplomacy is to persuade others, foreign policy should be able to identify and understand the motivations of why other people act in the way that they do. Thus, no diplomat should be working within a state if they do not fully understand the faiths that are active within that community.[65]

59 "Religion and Foreign Policy," in *Forgiveness and Reconciliation: Religion, Public Policy and Conflict Transformation*, ed. Raymond G. Helmick and Rodney Peterson, L. (Philadelphia: Templeton Foundation press, 2002).

60 R. Scott Appleby, "Retrieving the Missing Dimension of Statecraft: Religious Faith in the Service of Peacebuilding," in *Faith-Based Diplomacy: Trumping Realpolitik*, ed. Douglas M. Johnston (New York: Oxford University Press, 2003), 237.

61 Douglas M. Johnston, "Introduction: Real Politik Expanded," ibid., 7.

62 Madelaine Albright, "Faith and Diplomacy," *Review of Faith & International Affairs* 4, no. 2 (2006): 4.

63 The foundational text for this study is Douglas Johnston et al., *Religion, the Missing Dimension of Statecraft* (New York: Oxford University Press, 1994).

64 Sharp, "Crazy Religion Diplomacy," 255.

65 Albright, "Faith and Diplomacy," 8.

From this point, observers can recognise that inherent in religions is an authority to carry “traditions and methodologies that promote peace” and can be utilised to enhance the effectiveness of a diplomatic process.[66] This is the fundamental justification as to why diplomacy should consider faith. From this, there are several characteristics that make a faith-based approach to diplomacy distinct from other existing paradigms.

A fundamental principle of faith-based diplomacy is that it is oriented toward the divine. This means that there are transcendental assumptions that exist within humanity, identity and behaviour which impact conflict and also the effectiveness of diplomacy as a result.[67] Faith-based diplomacy, therefore, is distinguishable from other approaches to diplomacy because it inherently seeks to go beyond just stopping violent conflict, but rather seeks stop reconcile the relationships between parties to promote the potential of long-term positive peace.[68] This means that the framework of faith-based diplomacy cannot be seen as a classical tool of diplomacy, but is uniquely developed to address the concerns of contemporary conflict. Some other key goals include incorporating reconciliation and forgiveness into resolutions, to mediate estrangement, and to offer a viable avenue for affecting change in society.[69]

By the current frames of faith-based diplomacy, there are four areas faith-based diplomacy can be appropriately implemented, being:

1. In conflicts ‘in which religion is a significant factor in the identity of one or both communities’;
2. In conflict situations ‘in which religious leaders can be mobilized to facilitate peace’;
3. In situations in which ‘two major religious traditions [are] in a conflict that transcends national borders’; and

66 Sheherazade Jafari, “Local Religious Peacemakers: An Untapped Resource in U.S. Foreign Policy,” *Journal of International Affairs* 61, no. 1 (2007): 111.

67 Brian Cox and Daniel Philpott, “Faith-Based Diplomacy: An Ancient Idea Newly Emergent,” *Brandywine Review of Faith & International Affairs* 1, no. 2 (2003): 32.

68 Douglas M. Johnston and Brian Cox, “Faith-Based Diplomacy and Preventive Engagement,” in *Faith-Based Diplomacy: Trumping Realpolitik*, ed. Douglas M. Johnston (New York: Oxford University Press, 2003), 15 and Douglas M. Johnston, *Religion, Terror and Error: U.S. Foreign Policy and the Challenge of Spiritual Engagement* (California, United States: Praeger, 2011), 56.

69 Appleby, “Retrieving the Missing Dimension of Statecraft: Religious Faith in the Service of Peacebuilding,” 237 and Cecelia Lynch, “Christian Ethics, Actors, and Diplomacy: Mediating Universalist Pretentions,” *International Journal: Canada’s Journal of Global Policy Analysis* 66, no. 3 (2011): 615.

4. In 'third-party mediation in conflicts where there is no particular religious dimension present.'[70]

These are a helpful starting point for considering if a faith-based approach is an appropriate diplomatic strategy. However, an inherent concern when studying conflict is the fact that every conflict is unique, and thus the diplomatic approach must be tailored to appreciate the dynamics and nuances of the conflict case.[71] Operationally, however, the mechanisms and structures that can adequately incorporate faith-based diplomacy to address the concerns of intractable and identity-based conflicts are insufficient.[72]

2.2 *Defining Faith-based Diplomacy and the Faith-based Diplomat*

Defining faith-based diplomacy is important as it articulates the aims and goals of faith-based diplomacy as it has been proposed. These definitions also reveal central features of the faith-based approach to diplomacy which highlight its importance in the current system and its distinction from other forms of diplomacy. Scholars on the topic of faith-based diplomacy have generally been congruent in the definitions and main themes of faith-based diplomacy. In establishing the foundation for defining faith-based diplomacy, Appleby provides the central purpose of faith-based diplomacy, being that faith-based diplomacy "makes sense where religion is seen to be a genuine and in some cases a decisive factor in the conflict, rather than a dispensable sidebar ..."[73] Building on this aim, Johnston provides a simple definition that sets the scope for faith-based diplomacy, being:

> At the macro level, faith-based diplomacy simply means incorporating religious considerations into the practice of international politics. At the operational level, it involves making religion part of the solution to intractable, identity-based conflicts that escape the reach of traditional diplomacy. Typically these conflicts include an ethnic, tribal, or religious dimension.[74]

---

70 Jodok Troy, "Faith-Based Diplomacy under Examination," *The Hague Journal of Diplomacy* 3, no. 3 (2008): 218.

71 Douglas Johnston, "Review of the Findings," in *Religion, the Missing Dimension of Statecraft*, ed. Douglas Johnston and Cynthia Sampson (New York: Oxford University Press, 1994), 258.

72 Johnston, *Religion, Terror and Error: U.S. Foreign Policy and the Challenge of Spiritual Engagement*. 56.

73 Appleby, "Retrieving the Missing Dimension of Statecraft: Religious Faith in the Service of Peacebuilding," 238.

74 Johnston, *Religion, Terror and Error: U.S. Foreign Policy and the Challenge of Spiritual Engagement*. 56.

When investigating the concept within Diplomacy Studies, Cox and Philpott describe faith-based diplomacy as:

> 'track two,' that is, diplomacy practiced by non-state actors, officials of non-governmental organisations (NGOs), religious leaders and private citizens. Most distinctively, it is rooted in religions – their texts, their practices, their traditions, and the two-vectored spiritual orientation around which all of them revolve: first, the proper orientation of politics to the transcendent, and second, the active role of the divine in human affairs. Practitioners of faith-based diplomacy will, to be sure, draw upon secular expertise in conflict resolution and analysis, political science and philosophy, experience in national security, diplomacy, community development, and the like. But their central, orienting compass is their faith.[75]

This definition helps to frame faith-based diplomacy as it clearly identifies the actor typically engaged in the practice, the source of the concept's content, and its link to diplomacy. The categorisation of track two diplomacy is importantly referenced by most scholars in the field as non-state agents are typically the most appropriate to deliver this service. Troy suggests that track two agents are imperative as they work with the fundamental principles of faith-based diplomacy in that they focus on individual and community transformation, channelling personal beliefs and practices to address religious concerns.[76]

The definition that most succinctly encapsulates the meaning and purpose of faith-based diplomacy is Johnston and Cox's, a definition that is often used by others writing in the area. They define faith-based diplomacy as,

> … a form of Track II (unofficial) diplomacy that integrates the dynamics of religious faith with the conduct of international peacemaking. As such, it is more about reconciliation than it is conflict resolution. The peace that it pursues is not the mere absence of conflict but rather a restoration of healthy and respectful relationships between the parties.[77]

This definition has several notable features. The first is that the definition, consistent with earlier examples, promotes track two agents as the most effective agents for diplomacy in this area. The second feature reaffirms Johnston's

75 Cox and Philpott, "Faith-Based Diplomacy: An Ancient Idea Newly Emergent," 31-32.
76 Troy, "Faith-Based Diplomacy under Examination," 217-218.
77 Johnston and Cox, "Faith-Based Diplomacy and Preventive Engagement," 15.

goal stated earlier, that religious faith is actively incorporated as a central feature into the processes of peacemaking. The third feature in the definition is that faith-based diplomacy seeks to not just satisfy a negative peace, but rather go beyond the resolution of conflict and engage with reconciliation. Finally, the definition purports the aim of restoration of relationships as the primary goal of this diplomatic approach. While there are aspects of this definition that could be seen as a limiting factor, such as the agents able to engage in the process, it does accurately reflect the state of the theory as it currently stands.

Authors have not just engaged in how to define faith-based diplomacy, but to also set the parameters of what would constitute a faith-based diplomat. Several scholars have suggested central characteristics that would benefit the faith-based approach and suggested models for which this approach could best be taken. Appleby suggests that a faith-based diplomat can be viewed as a technical consult, a religious expert who could serve as a cultural attaché and support the diplomatic process in that way.[78] The literature surrounding how faith-based diplomats can be integrated into the diplomatic landscape is, however, quite limited. There is a constructive role for faith-based diplomats to engage as third-party mediators, but the training for diplomats outside of this model requires some re-evaluation. Religious peacemakers must be able to identify the participants from the community level who would be most effective in contributing positively to a peace process.[79] State governments must be able to understand the formal training of diplomats, but also review the processes of education and training for diplomatic and ambassadorial staff to ensure that they have a genuine understanding of the faiths practised within the countries that they are assigned.[80] This may be difficult considering the cost of training and the vast array of diplomatic posts that several countries have, but a strong beginning point is training diplomats and core specialists to work with key embassies, namely those that are representing states in zones where religious conflict does occur. These recommendations have been taken from Albright, who, during her time as the US Secretary of State, noticed this as a weakness of US diplomacy.[81] Even though the definitions and concepts of faith-based diplomacy focus on non-state actors as the prominent agents of faith-based diplomacy, these recommendations serve to highlight that there is potential for even traditional diplomats to become more 'faith-based' in their

78 R. Scott Appleby, "Retrieving the Missing Dimension of Statecraft: Religious Faith in the Service of Peacebuilding," ibid., 242.

79 Jafari, "Local Religious Peacemakers: An Untapped Resource in U.S. Foreign Policy," 125.

80 Albright, "Faith and Diplomacy," 8.

81 See ibid.

diplomatic approach. While the effective roles for faith-based diplomats are still being created, central qualities have been identified, underpinning how a faith-based diplomat should seek to act in the field.

Appleby writes that it is imperative that the faith-based diplomat be a person of faith who "understand the psychodynamics of religion and spirituality" because they have "experienced them personally and [have] meditated or reflected on them and their relevance to conflict transformation."[82] Building upon this core component of a faith-based diplomat, Johnston and Cox put forward five characteristics that faith-based diplomats require when engaging in diplomacy, being that:

1. There is a conscious dependency on spiritual principles and resources in the conduct of peacemaking;
2. They operate with a certain spiritual authority;
3. Have a pluralistic heart;
4. Have a transcendent approach to conflict resolution; and
5. Their ability to persevere against overwhelming odds.[83]

This frame for understanding a faith-based diplomat recognises the fundamental qualities that constitute religion and also a religious identity. This suggests that the faith-based diplomat understands the complex role of religion in conflict and can understand the practical nature of conflict among the people with an authority that can move communities toward peace.[84] Thompson also offers four central qualities that should be evident in a faith-based diplomat, being that:

1. They have a dependence on the divine and transcendent;
2. They treat perseverance and patience as imperatives into which they must grow in the diplomatic process and not as potential options;
3. They are aware of and weigh spiritual authority appropriately;
4. They have an awareness and knowledge of religious pluralism.[85]

These qualities reveal some important implications in the understanding of faith-based diplomacy. Not only does the diplomat rely on the divine, but they also engage with perseverance and patience. This is an important motivating factor that allows the diplomat to seek long-term solutions, but also inspire a level of hope in conflicts which have been intractable and ongoing

82 Appleby, "Retrieving the Missing Dimension of Statecraft: Religious Faith in the Service of Peacebuilding," 242.

83 Douglas M. Johnston and Brian Cox, "Faith-Based Diplomacy and Preventive Engagement," ibid., 16-17.

84 Jafari, "Local Religious Peacemakers: An Untapped Resource in U.S. Foreign Policy," 124-125.

85 Livingstone Thompson, "Religion and Diplomacy," *The Hague Journal of Diplomacy* 10, no. 2 (2015): 205-209.

for some time. Thompson's qualities of a faith-based diplomat also see that spiritual authority is a positive force, if used effectively, suggesting that the diplomat is aware that religious positions have been misused in the past to exacerbate conflict situations. The final characteristic offered by Thompson is integral to this paper, as the notion of religious pluralism is a fundamental position when engaging with not just faith-based diplomacy, but interfaith dialogue. This concept will be discussed in detail later in the paper, but this does point to an inherent complementarity between the concept of faith-based diplomacy and the practice of interfaith dialogue. With the defining scope of faith-based diplomacy now discussed, theoretical developments of faith-based diplomacy will be offered to present the support that already exists within Diplomacy Studies.

2.3 *The Scholarly Considerations of Faith-based Diplomacy*

When the theory of faith-based diplomacy was published in the 1990s, there was agreement among the authors at the time that a satisfactory framework for faith-based diplomacy existed.[86] However, considering the dramatic changes in the international system, and the literature that underpins those changes, faith-based diplomacy is in a position where it can be strengthened by the advancements made in the Diplomacy Studies. At the time, traditional frameworks for diplomacy were just adapted to integrate faith into their processes, but the methods were not able to accommodate those changes effectively.[87] The typical frame that would incorporate faith-based diplomacy is the rational-actor model, a model that suggests states are governed by the pursuit for self-interest and maximising their own power.[88] As traditional diplomacy has often been associated with the assumptions of the rational-actor model, it is apparent that religious and cultural dynamics of international affairs are deemed as irrational, and thus do not play a part in decision-making.[89] Considering religion as irrational, however, does not successfully deal with the impacts of religion, particularly in light of the nature of contemporary conflict. To counter this perspective, Johnston recommends that religion be viewed not as irrational, but as asymmetrical. This suggests that as an asymmetric threat,

86 Stanton Burnett, "Implications for the Foreign Policy Community," in *Religion, the Missing Dimension of Statecraft*, ed. Douglas & Sampson Johnston, Cynthia (New York: Oxford University Press, 1994), 296.

87 Douglas Johnston, "Looking Ahead: Toward a New Paradigm," ibid., ed. Douglas Johnston and Cynthia Sampson. 333.

88 Johnston, *Religion, Terror and Error: U.S. Foreign Policy and the Challenge of Spiritual Engagement*. 5.

89 Ibid., 5.

religion can be identified as a motivating force for behaviour and the religious nature of conflicting behaviours can be integrated into the decision-making calculus.[90] This type of change is evident in the way that nongovernmental and civil society organisations have been increasingly incorporated as actors in diplomacy. Agensky, upon evaluating religion's implications from the 19th century to the present, notes that religious scholarship has developed in the areas of aid, foreign policy, democratisation, security, rights, track two diplomacy and also in metatheoretical implications.[91] The traditional limitations and reticence for studying religion have weakened, with problematic assumptions about religion's place in international politics gradually dismantling, resulting in "a powerful new research agenda."[92] Promisingly, it is not just religion that can influence the processes of diplomacy. In fact, diplomatic values, principles and practices can also enhance religious activities. This enhanced research agenda can generate the mutual enrichment of these two systems.

When considering the linkage between faith-based diplomacy and the metatheories of International Relations, religion has found a role as a variable in explanatory theory in that it can bring some understanding as to what is happening in other parts of the world.[93] From this basis, Sandal and James studied how religion links with realism, liberalism, neorealism and neoliberalism to find which theoretical lens is most appropriate in clarifying the place of religion. As classical realism focuses on the state as the unitary proponent of power, religion is only really understood through the lens of the state insofar as it impacts both human nature and power.[94] That being said, the work done by the English School in the latter stages of the 20th century did provide a more meaningful frame of analysis for religion even within this classical perspective.[95] Neorealism, however, does not comfortably accommodate religion other than understanding it as a motivation for actors' behaviour with Sandal and James concluding that neorealism is the most challenging framework for religion to be applied within. Nonetheless, the authors do concede that there is still potential for models to be created in this paradigm to show the

90 "An Asymmetric Counter to the Asymmetric Threat," 9.

91 Jonathan C. Agensky, "Recognizing Religion: Politics, History, and the 'Long 19th Century'," *European Journal of International Relations* 23, no. 4 (2017): 732.

92 Ibid., 748.

93 Nukhet A. Sandal and Patrick James, "Religion and International Relations Theory: Towards a Mutual Understanding," ibid., 17, no. 1 (2011): 4.

94 Ibid., 18.

95 Lynch, "Christian Ethics, Actors, and Diplomacy: Mediating Universalist Pretentions," 616.

value of faith and religion in international affairs in the future.[96] The liberal perspectives are more accommodating for the role of religion. Neoliberalism sees religion as a way for transnational actors to pursue their own goals, to build cultural norms and explanations of politics based on the tools within the liberal tradition.[97] Neoliberalism is the most obvious theoretical lens to apply to fully understand the place of religion in international affairs as it accounts for religious institutions, their transnational implications, and ways to understand how religion fits within mainstream international affairs.[98] While this discussion of metatheory may help clarify the perspectives that can be taken to understand religion, Agensky notes that incorporating faith-based approaches into international relations scholarship is limited by a secularist outlook to theory development, with scholars maintaining Eurocentric assumptions of religion in politics, often relegating religious actors and beliefs as 'the other' in international affairs.[99] Still, this analysis demonstrates that there is room for religion to be appreciated in the frames of International Relations metatheory.

Narrowing further to the scope to Diplomacy Studies, Sharp suggests, "all religious thought offers an opening in principle at least, to diplomacy."[100] While politics and religion generally remain as separate entities, there are values, principles and norms that do overlap when examining diplomacy and religion. Bloweski suggests that from the practitioner's viewpoint, the civilizing mission and social practices of diplomacy look toward dialogue, engagement, empathy, principled pragmatism, restraint for the sake of harmonisation, and awareness of the context of global issues, among others.[101] In contrast to this, religious ethics that inform social practice rely on spiritual authority, compassion, reconciliation, forgiveness, peace, religious education and identities. The spaces where these notions converge are areas in which successful strategy can be developed. Harmonising these two systems, religion and diplomacy, will allow for the goals and aims of faith-based diplomacy and interfaith dialogue to be more successful. Thinking of the traditional school of diplomacy, religious structures and mechanisms that would relate to diplomacy were withdrawn into the interior of the state as diplomatic actors became more secular

96 Sandal and James, "Religion and International Relations Theory: Towards a Mutual Understanding," 12-18.

97 Ibid., 15-17.

98 Ibid., 19.

99 Jonathan C. Agensky, "Recognizing Religion: Politics, History, and the 'Long 19th Century'," ibid., 23, no. 4 (2017): 732-748.

100 Sharp, "Crazy Religion Diplomacy," 244.

101 See Wilfried Bolewski, "Corporate Diplomacy as Global Management," *International Journal of Diplomacy and Economy* 4, no. 2 (2018).

while the international elite assumed that religion would just remain in this way into the future.[102] While faith-based diplomacy has been suggested as a way to understand the place of religion in the contemporary system, Albright cautions that it cannot replace traditional diplomacy altogether, but rather those who construct policy should balance the influence of religion with traditional decision-making approaches.[103] Johnston supports this claim suggesting that faith-based diplomacy can be seen as an additional resource in the arsenal of a diplomat's available strategies.[104] Beyond traditional diplomacy, the new and innovative schools of diplomacy see a clear interaction with faith-based diplomacy. International organisations, nonstate actors, religious groups and even religious individuals have found a way to the table, and these diplomatic actors often seek ways to integrate faith favourably.[105] Incorporating actors through the multiple tracks of diplomacy has ultimately changed the architecture surrounding diplomatic engagement and has provided more opportunity for faith-based actors to be a part of the diplomatic process.[106]

With specific reference to theories in Diplomacy Studies, two theoretical lenses are complementary to the addition of faith-based diplomacy. They are cultural diplomacy and public diplomacy. In cultural diplomacy, using culture as a way to engage and understand different groups is a practice that has occurred through history, but only emerged in scholarship in the 1990s.[107] As religion and culture often have a symbiotic relationship with society, the two areas can be seen as variables in the diplomatic decision-making model, able to play a determining role in policy outcomes.[108] Religion is an influential element in culture, and thus if cultural diplomacy strategies are to be employed, religion should be a consideration of the planning and implementation of these diplomatic strategies.[109]

---

102 Sharp, "Crazy Religion Diplomacy," 259.

103 Albright, "Faith and Diplomacy," 9.

104 Quoted in Loramy Gerstbauer, "Faith in Religion's Reconciling Power," *Brandywine Review of Faith & International Affairs* 2, no. 2 (2004): 50.

105 Johnston, "Introduction: Beyond Power Politics," 3-4 and Thomas Diez, "Diplomacy, Papacy, and the Transformation of International Society," *The Review of Faith & International Affairs* 15, no. 4 (2017): 34.

106 Troy, "Faith-Based Diplomacy under Examination," 227-228.

107 Charlotte Faucher, "Cultural Diplomacy and International Cultural Relations in Twentieth-Century Europe," *Contemporary European History* 25, no. 2 (2016): 374.

108 Ganesh Prasad Pokhariyal, "The Influence of Religion, Technology, and Economy on Culture, Diplomacy, and Peace," *International Journal on World Peace* 32, no. 2 (2015): 42.

109 Philip Seib, "Introduction," in *Religion and Public Diplomacy*, ed. Philip Seib (New York: Palgrave Macmillan, 2013), 7.

An area of diplomatic study that has developed a strong appreciation of religious considerations is public diplomacy. The text *Religion and Public Diplomacy*, edited by Philip Seib, is an example of how the literature is expanding to find areas of complementarity between these two ideas.[110] In a simple form, public diplomacy is a diplomatic strategy that attracts and influences foreign publics – one way to do this is through the faith of the people in those communities.[111] Discourse is the central feature of public diplomacy, and as a result, the focus of public diplomacy becomes people, not just institutions.[112] These features become more complicated when integrating the myriad of actors and modes, including social media and communication technologies present in the current environment. It is known that identity, norms and beliefs are all concepts informed and reinforced by religion, but they are also ideas that can play an important place in enhancing the credibility and legitimacy of policies in the public diplomacy lens.[113] One area of intersection that has featured heavily in the development of public diplomacy is that of religious freedom. Religious freedom can work to satisfy three strategic objectives of public diplomacy, being "shaping the narrative, expanding and strengthening people-to-people trust, and combatting violent extremism."[114] As public diplomacy strategies are able to consider theologies and worldviews, public diplomacy becomes a more successful vehicle for promoting and protecting religious freedom when traditional mechanisms are unsuccessful.[115] This example of religious freedom, and even the goals and strategies of public diplomacy demonstrate that there is a level of complementarity with faith-based diplomacy and can be used as a platform to develop credible and effective faith-based approaches.

2.4 *Actors and Agents of Faith-based Diplomacy*

As alluded to throughout this section, there are important considerations to be made when selecting the most effective actors to engage in faith-based diplomacy. While the definitions and theoretical analysis suggest that faith-based

110 See P. Seib, *Religion and Public Diplomacy* (Palgrave Macmillan US, 2013).

111 Huston Smith, *The Illustrated World's Religions: A Guide to Our Wisdom Traditions* (San Francisco: Harper Collins, 1994).

112 Burnett, "Implications for the Foreign Policy Community," 296 and Philip Seib, "Religious Freedom and Us Public Diplomacy," *Review of Faith & International Affairs* 11, no. 1 (2013): 15.

113 Ben D. Mor, "Credibility Talk in Public Diplomacy," *Review of International Studies* 38, no. 2 (2012): 418.

114 Liora Danan, "A Public Diplomacy Approach to International Religious Freedom," *Review of Faith & International Affairs* 10, no. 3 (2012): 60.

115 Ibid., 59.

diplomacy is an activity conducted by track two agents of diplomacy, there is merit in examining how other actors may engage in the practice. Typically, the state views religion as an internal affair and thus does not intervene in conflicts of a religious nature. This has resulted in individuals and non-state actors having to fill the gaps left by the state in this space, leaving non-state actors have often been the primary diplomatic agents,[116] as evident in the areas of education, health services and emergency relief. This does not, however, mean that the state does not have a place to engage in faith-based diplomacy. States often marginalise religion as a cultural issue and government departments reflect that in that their political structures diminish any sense of priority toward religious considerations.[117] The government diplomat has had to work within these structures. While many call for diplomats to be trained to better understand the trends of religion, progress to accomplish these types of changes is often slow within the state machinery. At its core though, the state can offer some role in facilitating faith-based diplomacy. As Danforth suggests, "diplomats are trained to address political rather than religious disputes … but while government officials cannot do the work of religion, they can create conditions under which that work can be done."[118]

Nonstate actors working within track two diplomacy are naturally better equipped to engage in faith-based diplomacy. However, the structures within the institution of diplomacy remain state-centric and need to adjust to allow for nonstate actors to play a more meaningful role in the diplomatic process.[119] There are a number of diplomatic services that nonstate actors can deliver, and they should be evaluated when constructing strategy. From a theoretical lens, the English School provides an analytical framework to see religion as a 'hybrid actor,' wherein diplomatic actors represent both states and religions.[120] In this categorisation, religion will be better understood as a form of world society that can influence foreign policy and transnational issues. This analysis suggests that the 'actorness' of religion is being constructed to more effectively engage in the structures of the international system. While intergovernmental organisations are impacting the diplomatic landscape, such as the United Nations and multilateral diplomatic engagement, these institutions are

116 Johnston, "Introduction: Beyond Power Politics," 3-4.

117 Thomas F. Farr, "Diplomacy in an Age of Faith," *Foreign Affairs* 87, no. 2 (2008). And Johnston, *Religion, Terror and Error: U.S. Foreign Policy and the Challenge of Spiritual Engagement.* 84.

118 John Danforth, "Mobilizing Religion against Terrorism," *Brown Journal of World Affairs* 24, no. 1 (2017): 83.

119 Johnston, "Religion and Foreign Policy."

120 McLarren and Stahl, "'Hybrid Actors' – Religion and the Shift Towards a World Society".

beholden to the interests of member states and the structures of the intergovernmental organisation. There is, however, within these structures the potential for normative values and pluralism to be supported and strengthened diplomatically.[121] Some intergovernmental organisations have promoted programs that invite religious dialogue, but this can quickly change depending on the support and interests of the member states and potential changes in the international agenda.

The nonstate actors that have the most potential for working with faith-based diplomacy are nongovernmental and faith-based civil society organisations. This is as they have a positive relationship with their communities that allow them to naturally engage with humanitarian assistance and community reconstruction, for example.[122] The environment of multi-stakeholder collaboration, where more actors are being invited to diplomatic activities, has become more prominent as a result.[123] Nongovernmental organisations are the primary actor to fill the gaps left by the state, especially in cases where the state ignores the place of religion. Faith-based nongovernmental organisations are able to, as Johnston posits, "exploit their religious identities, relationships of trust, and far-reaching networks" to offer an integral tool for conflict mitigation.[124] The network of faith-based non-governmental organisations, the way these organisations work closely with the community, and the focus of organisations to deliver specific services means that these actors can identify the deeper motivators of conflict, rebuild communal relationships and work to provide long-term resolutions to conflict.[125]

Civil society organisations and places of worship are also uniquely positioned to support faith-based diplomacy efforts. Civil society provides an avenue for democratic participation from many walks of life and works to balance the power of the state as it reflects to society, with civil society agents often working closely with religious bodies to affect political change.[126] Due to their structure and communal involvement, civil society organisations have a

121 Mario Mauro, "Religious Aspects of Politics," *European View* 11, no. 2 (2012).

122 Marsden, "Faith-Based Diplomacy: Conservative Evangelicals and the United States Military," 494.

123 Eugene K. B. Tan, "Faith, Freedom, and Us Foreign Policy: Avoiding the Proverbial Clash of Civilizations in East and Southeast Asia," *Review of Faith & International Affairs* 11, no. 1 (2013): 76-77.

124 Johnston, *Religion, Terror and Error: U.S. Foreign Policy and the Challenge of Spiritual Engagement*. 148.

125 "Religion and Foreign Policy."

126 Cox and Philpott, "Faith-Based Diplomacy: An Ancient Idea Newly Emergent," 36-37.

key voice in intellectual, institutional, market and political spaces.[127] This suggests that civil society organisations have a vast network of avenues by which diplomatic strategies can be channelled. Faith-based civil society organisations represent every major world religion and are now spread across the globe, making civil society a "strategic site for faith-based diplomacy."[128] Not only are civil society organisations important in affecting change at the grassroots level, but they can also influence leaders, by virtue of their role and membership, to pursue the goals of faith-based diplomacy such as reconciliation.[129] Because these faith-based civil society organisations are motivated by religious values, they are able to offer support and deliver services which are often viewed by the community as credible, legitimate and justified, including delivering humanitarian assistance as part of a diplomatic program for example.[130]

The most apparent and well-established institution to play an integral role in the faith-based approach is the community of faith and places of worship. Johnston identifies some key ways in which places of worship can be integral agents in diplomacy. Firstly, there is an inherent influence of the church[131] within the community as, in the eyes of the population, it may be the only institution with moral legitimacy.[132] Due to this, there are five key ways the church can contribute to peace, being:

1. An established record for humanitarian care and concern;
2. A respected set of values, including a reputation for trustworthiness;
3. Unique leverage for promoting reconciliation between conflicting parties;
4. A capability for mobilising community, national, and international support for a peace process;
5. An ability to follow through locally in the wake of a settlement.[133]

As with most considerations in faith-based diplomacy, even the church can unfortunately play an exacerbating role in conflict, with examples of the church supporting violence and human rights abuses being commonly observed.

---

127 John D. Brewer, Gareth I. Higgins, and Francis Teeney, "Religion and Peacemaking: A Conceptualization," *Sociology* 44, no. 6 (2010): 1024-1025.

128 Albright, "Faith and Diplomacy," 8 and Cox and Philpott, "Faith-Based Diplomacy: An Ancient Idea Newly Emergent," 36-37.

129 "Faith-Based Diplomacy: An Ancient Idea Newly Emergent," 36-37.

130 Fredy Munthe, "Religious Movements in Humanitarian Issue: The Emergence of Faith-Based Organizations (Fbo) in Diplomacy Sphere," *Jurnal Hubangan Internasional* 5, no. 2 (2016): 176.

131 When the author refers to 'church' they mean places of worship generally which may include mosques, temples, synagogues etc. The term reflects the referenced author's choice of term in the research.

132 Johnston, "Review of the Findings," 260-261.

133 Ibid., 262.

However, if incorporated effectively, these organisations can have a significant role in civil society to promote and support a peace process in the community.

2.5 *Key Concepts of Faith-based Diplomacy*

This final section of analysis regarding faith-based diplomacy will propose some of the positive aspects of faith-based diplomacy that are consistent across the literature. These will be given here to suggest some areas of opportunity that those in the theory and practice of diplomacy can utilise in the diplomatic programs they develop in the future. The first is the asset of values that can be found in faith which provide support underpinning a peace process. Religious beliefs and values can motivate behaviour, and if integrated cohesively into the community, they can assist in lessening conflict.[134] Incorporating religious values into the construction and dialogue of a peace process can fit within the 'virtue ethics' approach of diplomacy, as discussed by Troy.[135] The values are drawn from the rich tradition of religions, namely scriptural texts, which can be used to substantiate the processes working toward peaceful resolution.[136] Some pertinent values identified in literature include language, hospitality, trust, forgiveness, and love – some of these being useful considerations in interfaith approaches to dialogue discussed later in the paper.

A growing trend in conflict resolution and diplomacy is reconciliation, a concept that is deeply embedded in several religious traditions. It is an important aspect of addressing the deep constructs of identity, and thus as can be a powerful counter to identity conflict.[137] The value of reconciliation can be found in several religious traditions with the language surrounding reconciliation often having substantial meaning. Due to this rich depth, reconciliation is a key feature of the central definition of faith-based diplomacy. In fact, reconciliation is so integral within faith that Troy concludes "faith-based diplomacy is more about reconciliation than conflict resolution."[138] In a practical sense, reconciliation within faith-based diplomacy can manifest in five different ways, including:

1. Unity in diversity through active acceptance of the pluralistic nature of life itself regarding race, gender, ethnicity, and culture;

134 Edward Luttwak, "The Missing Dimension," ibid., ed. Douglas & Sampson Johnston, Cynthi, 17.

135 Troy, "Faith-Based Diplomacy under Examination."

136 Johnston, *Religion, Terror and Error: U.S. Foreign Policy and the Challenge of Spiritual Engagement*. 38.

137 Cox and Philpott, "Faith-Based Diplomacy: An Ancient Idea Newly Emergent," 34.

138 Troy, "Faith-Based Diplomacy under Examination," 228.

2. The inclusion of all parties in any final solution, including one's enemies wherever possible;
3. The peaceful resolution of the conflict between individuals and groups;
4. Forgiveness as a prerequisite for restoring healthy relationships; and,
5. Social justice as the appropriate basis for a right ordering of relationships.[139]

Finding that intersection between reconciliation and faith-based diplomacy will inevitably support the conflict resolution strategies which seek reconciliation after conflict. This is a significant opportunity for advancement in this field.

In the purview of diplomacy, individuals are being considered as potential diplomatic actors in their own accord. Within faith-based diplomacy, the role of individual agents is most evident through religious leaders, as they are becoming increasingly recognised at various levels of the peace process. Two fundamental reasons support why religious leaders can be a valuable asset in diplomacy. The first is that religious leaders can validate the peace process and sustain peace after negotiations, and the second is that religious leaders can persuade groups to work together which requires a level of authority on religious issues.[140] The presence of religious leaders at the negotiating table contributes to providing a mechanism for engagement, methods of communication, assistance to diplomatic procedures, and an intermediary between competing claims.[141] Religious leaders can positively influence a peace process as they have:

1. A well-established and pervasive influence in the community;
2. A reputation as an apolitical force for change based on a respected set of values;
3. Unique social leverage for reconciling conflicting parties, including an ability to rehumanize relationships;
4. The capability to mobilise community, national, and international support for a peace process.[142]

For these reasons, the religious leader can be a vital part in sustaining a peace process by translating diplomatic objectives to the community. Religious leaders also have a significant influence on the general public as they mediate a progressive humanism that pursues social justice. This encourages religious leaders, and their communities, to provide services for the community that legitimise religious activities within society. Ultimately, this is a powerful force

139 Johnston and Cox, "Faith-Based Diplomacy and Preventive Engagement," 16.
140 Albright, "Faith and Diplomacy," 9.
141 Luttwak, "The Missing Dimension," 17.
142 Johnston and Cox, "Faith-Based Diplomacy and Preventive Engagement," 14.

that can be utilised within faith-based diplomacy, but also the practices of faith-based diplomacy – including interfaith dialogue.

The final area of opportunity for faith-based diplomacy discussed in this section is the capacity for a faith-based diplomat to engage as a third-party mediator. Whether in an official capacity or as a nonofficial track two agent, third-party mediators are becoming a more prominent strategy of negotiations and conflict resolution.[143] As a mediator, faith-based actors can provide a negotiating mechanism, procedure, and format for communication but most importantly, they are able to present themselves as an 'insider-partial' mediator which means they are engaged in the mediation process not from a distance, but rather because they have trusted relationships with the conflict parties and a desire to achieve peace.[144] These faith-based representatives have longstanding relationships that are often able to transcend the boundaries of traditional politics and thus provide renewed momentum to potentially stagnated negotiations.[145] The prime example of this occurring is how the Pope was a third-party mediator to the negotiations between Cuba and the US in 2014.[146] As the role for third-party mediators continues to become established in the practices of conflict resolution and diplomacy, religious actors can be more seriously considered for this position. Within the scope of mediation, faith-based mediation is garnering academic attention, with scholars highlighting the potential for improved conflict resolution strategies when faith-based actors are integrated into mediation.[147] These advancements in other areas of study show promising trends for strengthening the inclusion of faith in diplomacy.

The integration of faith into diplomacy is a perspective in diplomatic theory that has been gaining traction in recent decades. Further to this is an area of great promise in the future of faith-based diplomacy, being the development of interfaith dialogue. Interestingly, interfaith dialogue has not been fully considered as a viable strategy within diplomatic literature, but its compatibility with the goals of faith-based diplomacy, and diplomacy more broadly suggest

143 Johnston, "Introduction: Beyond Power Politics," 4.

144 Luttwak, "The Missing Dimension," 17 and Bruce Nichols, "Religious Conciliation between the Sandinistas and the East Coast Indians of Nicaragua," ibid., ed. Douglas Johnston and Cynthia Sampson, 72.

145 "Religious Conciliation between the Sandinistas and the East Coast Indians of Nicaragua," 82.

146 See "US and Cuba: Remaking of a Relationship," *Strategic Comments* 21, no. 3 (2015).

147 See Jacob Bercovitch and Ayse S. Kadayifci-Orellana, "Religion and Mediation: The Role of Faith-Based Actors in International Conflict Resolution," *International Negotiation* 14, no. 1 (2009).

that it is an area worth investigating. In fact, scholars see the link between interfaith dialogue and faith-based diplomacy, noting that interfaith dialogue engages with peacemaking through reconciling religious tensions.[148] Prominent world leaders have made statements that highlight the importance of dialogue between faith communities, including Obama's 2009 Cairo address and "Pope Francis's 2013 speech in Argentina, wherein he said that, when difficulties arise, his advice was: 'dialogue, dialogue, dialogue!' "[149]

Currently, there is a distinction between the two areas of study. Within scholarship, one fits predominantly within Diplomacy Studies while the other exists traditionally through comparative theology and biblical studies. Not only is there difference between scholarship and theory, but there is also a difference in practice. This is most notable when considering the actors that engage in the faith-based diplomacy and interfaith dialogue. Typically, faith-based diplomacy involves the state and religious communities where both sides incorporate their respective principles and procedures into a diplomatic process to solve pressing concerns. Interfaith dialogue focuses on religious communities as nonstate actors where the state may mediate and use that position to offer diplomatic principles and procedures. Interfaith dialogue then engages with a myriad of actors to achieve community projects, reconciliation and peacemaking initiatives. Even though these distinctions exist, there are opportunities to build on the convergent goals of faith-based diplomacy and interfaith dialogue and find ways where the actors can work cooperatively. The effective operationalization of interfaith strategies can substantiate the progress achieved in faith-based diplomacy and provide policy-makers with innovative perspectives to address future challenges.

3 Interfaith Dialogue

The central purpose of this paper is to present the models of interfaith dialogue that have been promoted in other areas of study to highlight their potential as a method of faith-based diplomacy, enhancing the perspective of faith in diplomacy more broadly. Potentially the most famous turning point in the study and practice of interfaith dialogue came in the 1990s when Professor Hans Küng proposed the Foundation for a Global Ethic, wherein he articulated

148 T. Kayaoglu, "Explaining Interfaith Dialogue in the Muslim World," *Politics and Religion* 8, no. 2 (2015): 237.

149 Swidler, "Sorting out Meanings: 'Religion,' 'Spiritual,' 'Interreligious,' 'Interfaith,' Etc.," 383.

a theological basis for engaging in dialogue.[150] Many observers quote this as the foundation for interfaith dialogue – Küng's famous formula, being:

- No peace among the nations without peace among the religions.
- No peace among the religions without dialogue between the religions.
- No dialogue between the religions without investigation of the foundations of the religions.[151]

This formulation aptly presents the reason why pursuing this area of inquiry is so important, potentially even more so in today's political climate than when it was offered before the turn of the century.

In conceptualising interfaith dialogue within the diplomatic scope of analysis, Hames suggests that this process is essentially a form of politics as "it demands negotiating the barriers between different faiths in order to be able to undermine those from within who are abusing it."[152] This requires, in practice, that participants simplify their positions to the simplest form to improve human cooperation.[153] But the literature on interfaith dialogue, much less the policies that target interfaith relations, "lacks any scope for genuinely political relationships or any account of how interfaith relations are affected by the market and the state."[154] The exploration of interfaith dialogue still sits within a narrow scope of analysis which is limiting its potential, particularly as a strategy of diplomacy. Research conducted on interfaith practices, namely in the United States, interrogates attempts at achieving communicative objectives, with the practice of interfaith dialogue focusing on collaborative practices, shared rituals or integrating theological constructions into individual life.[155] This is the basic research approach for interfaith dialogue that can be developed further to more closely align with the goals of diplomacy.

This is a real possibility as increasingly observers recognise the complementary elements interfaith dialogue shares with other disciplines, such as conflict resolution, education, communication and so on.[156] For example,

150 See Hans Küng, *A Global Ethic for Global Politics and Economics* (Oxford University Press, 1997).

151 As cited in Magonet, "The Growth of Interfaith Dialogue," 41.

152 Harvey Hames, "How Do Conflict Situations Affect Our Faith Communities and Our Interreligious Relationships?," ibid., 37, no. 1 (2004): 74.

153 Ibid., 74.

154 Bretherton, "A Postsecular Politics? Inter-Faith Relations as a Civic Practice," 346.

155 Terry Shoemaker and James Edmonds, "The Limits of Interfaith? Interfaith Identities, Emerging Potentialities, and Exclusivity," *Culture and Religion* 17, no. 2 (2016): 201.

156 See, for an example of this interdisciplinary approach, Claire Holland and Marney Walker, "Choice Theory and Interfaith Dialogue: Building Relationships between Faiths and Embracing Diversity," *International Journal of Choice Theory & Reality Therapy* 37, no. 2 (2018).

Irmgedruth notes that religion and culture are two forces that work closely in society to develop group identities, and thus understanding that religion can shape culture and that culture can shape religion is an important notion when looking for different perspectives to incorporate religion into peacebuilding initiatives.[157] Miller identifies the need for interfaith dialogue to be incorporated into management practices.[158] Pallavincini highlights that the interfaith components of religious education are an important area of development.[159] Higher education and secondary schools have worked to improve programs on diversity, but content should be improved to highlight interfaith leadership, religious diversity and the impact these values have on democracy.[160] With interfaith approaches being incorporated into the practices of various fields, the potential for the natural translation of interfaith dialogue into diplomacy can be realised.

3.1 *Definitions of Interfaith Dialogue*

Earlier in this paper, the concept of dialogue was defined. At this juncture, fully exploring the definition and defining features of interfaith diplomacy will help scope the remaining analysis in this paper. At its core, interfaith dialogue seeks to serve as a counter effort to group fears and religious violence, which then liberates and empowers religious groups.[161] The simple starting point of Interfaith dialogue relates to attitudes, judgements and appreciations of other faiths.[162] This basic premise underpins the development of more specific definitions for interfaith dialogue.

Similar to the definitions of religion and faith, some scholars choose to refer to this process as interreligious dialogue. A definition provided for

157 Rainer B. Irmgedruth, "The Religious Challenge: To Live in the Context of Diverse Cultures," *European Judaism* 37, no. 1 (2004): 57.

158 See Kent D. Miller, "Interfaith Dialogue in a Secular Field," *Management Research Review* 40, no. 8 (2017). This follows trends in diplomacy more broadly, where observers note the growing influence of transnational corporations in the area of foreign policy. See Bolewski, "Corporate Diplomacy as Global Management."

159 See Yahya Pallavicini, "Interfaith Education: An Islamic Perspective," *International Review of Education / Internationale Zeitschrift für Erziehungswissenschaft* 62, no. 4 (2016).

160 Several specific examples are documented in Eboo Patel, "Preparing Interfaith Leaders: Knowledge Base and Skill Set for Interfaith Leaders," *New Directions for Student Leadership* 2016, no. 152 (2016): 76.

161 Siti Sarah Muwahidah, "Interfaith Dialogue at the Grassroots Level: A Case Study of an Interfaith Empowerment Program in East Java, Indonesia," *Political Theology* 9, no. 1 (2008): 86.

162 Adrianus Sunarko Ofm, "Interfaith Dialogue and Cooperation across Faiths: The Experience of Indonesia," *Theology Today* 73, no. 1 (2016): 58.

interreligious dialogue suggests that there are two interconnected purposes of dialogue. The first is "to overcome ignorance and prejudice, fostering mutual understanding among the religions" and the second is "to discover the values held in common by these religions, making possible cooperation in support of the common good."[163] In simpler terms, Merdjanova defines interreligious dialogue as "human communication between religious leaders for the primary purpose of clarifying theological/philosophical similarities and differences," but expands on this definition to highlight the potential for "mutual understanding and cooperation between people who self-identify religiously."[164] Because interreligious dialogue refers to the process of exchange between groups defined by religious traditions, it does not have the same inherent limitations in meaning as the terms religion and faith do. For that reason, the term interreligious and interfaith will be used to reflect the literature examined through this paper. However, consistent with earlier sections, interfaith dialogue will be preferred.

Another term that is increasingly linked with interfaith dialogue is the notion of intra-faith dialogue. This concept recognises that there can be multiple communities within one religious tradition, and the differences between those groups may also need to be addressed, particularly when considering the communal nature of some conflicts.[165] Recently, this has become a necessary strategy within the Islamic community, as 'inter-Muslim dialogue' can present intellectual progress and spiritual stimulation between parties that settle internal disputes, then acting as a framework to apply to different religious groups in the West.[166] This process is more important for minority Muslim communities within the West who see inter-Muslim dialogue as a tool with great potential for enhancing peace.[167] Essentially this term highlights the need to not only engage in dialogue with religious groups outside of one's own, but to also be mindful of the needs, positions and interests of one's own religious group to ensure that communication and representation are still being achieved. Importantly, achieving the goals of intra-faith dialogue will also serve, by extension, to strengthen the outcomes of interfaith dialogue.

Some challenges are present when defining interfaith dialogue. Although there is now a mainstream understanding in contemporary theology that

163 Baum, "Interreligious Dialogue Includes Listening to Secular Voices," 363.

164 Ina Merdjanova, "Overhauling Interreligious Dialogue for Peacebuilding," *Occasional Papers on Religion in Eastern Europe* 36, no. 1 (2016): 27.

165 Neufeldt, "Interfaith Dialogue: Assessing Theories of Change," 364.

166 Kemal Argon, "Strategies for Interreligious and Inter-Muslim Dialogue: A Proposed Methodology," *Journal of Muslim Minority Affairs* 29, no. 3 (2009): 355.

167 Ibid., 366.

dialogue between traditions is necessary, there is no "common understanding of the character and purpose of such dialogue."[168] This is why defining not only interfaith dialogue but also the purpose for interfaith dialogue, is an important element of its success. Furthermore, Swidler notes that while the term 'interfaith' resonates with the Abrahamic religious traditions as faith is a central characteristic of their religious teachings, other world religions – namely Eastern religious traditions – do not share the same immediate connection with the term.[169] These cautions must be taken into account when evaluating the definition of interfaith dialogue.

Suomala describes interfaith dialogue as a 20th century development primarily in the West which "involves more structured and formal conversations between representatives (usually religious scholars, clergy, and institutional officials) from at least two clearly defined religious traditions with the primary objective of mutual understanding rather than conversion."[170] This definition provides the practical form of the process. Expanding on the content of interfaith dialogue, Eck notes that even though there are a variety of definitions provided for interfaith dialogue, there are consistent themes presented. Those themes are the mutuality of speaking and listening, dialogue that penetrates superficial encounters, a genuine openness to discuss concerns, and the desire to be heard.[171] Whether the concept of dialogue is applied to everyday life, learning, community issues, faith and theology, those central aspects remain apparent across the definitions of interfaith dialogue.

3.2 *The Goals of Interfaith Dialogue*

To clarify the main purpose of interfaith dialogue as part of the promotion of peace efforts within the wider political environment, Neufeldt quotes the Tirana Declaration, which sets out the goals of interfaith dialogue in achieving peace. The Declaration states "We hold that dialogue must be conducted on a platform of democracy, the rule of law and respect for human rights and dignity of the individual," and that "all faiths convey a message of peace, justice and human solidarity" which informs how people act within society.[172] This recognises the inherent potential of interfaith dialogue whereby genuine

168 Patrik Fridlund, "Double Religious Belonging and Some Commonly Held Ideas About Dialogue and Conversion," *Mission Studies: Journal of the International Association for Mission Studies* 31, no. 2 (2014): 256.

169 Swidler, "Sorting out Meanings: 'Religion,' 'Spiritual,' 'Interreligious,' 'Interfaith,' Etc.," 380.

170 Suomala, "Complex Religious Identity in the Context of Interfaith Dialogue," 360-361.

171 Diana Eck, "Interfaith Dialogue in the New Religious America," *Review & Expositor* 114, no. 1 (2017): 27.

172 Neufeldt, "Interfaith Dialogue: Assessing Theories of Change," 357.

change can be achieved in society to enhance peace. However, the true success of interfaith dialogue is not in simply using dialogue as a way to debate issues of doctrine, or finding a 'lowest common denominator' between religious traditions, or even just to identify areas of convergence between religious traditions.[173] These may be helpful starting points, and have often been the main focus of interfaith dialogue in the past, but they do not fully encapsulate the powerful impact that interfaith dialogue can have in the community. Genuine dialogue works to develop understanding, of the individual participant firstly, but also of their interlocutors.[174] It also demands that listening occurs between groups, which results in what Hunt suggests is the ultimate aim of interfaith dialogue, being "hearing through each others' ears and hearts."[175] What this encourages is a deeper exchange between individuals that goes beyond superficial understandings of religion and moves toward an appreciation of identity. When this is understood, the motivations and desires leading to conflict can be more accurately identified and hopefully mitigated.

The goals of interfaith dialogue may also vary depending on the context, region, or religious position being represented in the dialogue. For example, the goals of interfaith dialogue from a Muslim perspective are "to foster improved relations with non-Muslim communities, primarily in the West, to foster and enhance relations between minority Muslim communities, and ultimately for Muslims to revivify their own local communities."[176] Understanding the context enables a more appropriate model for interfaith dialogue to be employed. Building on this, another main purpose of interfaith dialogue, as put forward by Hames, is for different religious systems, "to accept responsibility for the consequences of our acts, to promote tolerance, educate to the possibility of a plurality of interpretations, and encourage dialogue," which, when applied to the context of terrorism and conflict, "if unable to sway fundamentalism, will at least cut away its grassroots support and minimise recruitment to its ranks."[177] This is an imperative goal as some observers suggest that fundamentalism is the most significant development in modern religion as it is a transforming force within most major religions around the world, and yet interfaith dialogue

173 Anne Hunt, "Interfaith Dialogue: Lessons from the Ecumenical Movement," *Compass* 44, no. 1 (2010): 8-9.

174 Ibid., 9.

175 Ibid., 9.

176 Argon, "Strategies for Interreligious and Inter-Muslim Dialogue: A Proposed Methodology," 355.

177 Hames, "How Do Conflict Situations Affect Our Faith Communities and Our Interreligious Relationships?," 74.

often ignored these developments.[178] Huff, in 2000, stated that interfaith dialogue "will never fulfil its unique mission until it recognised the fundamentalisms of the world" as necessary to dialogue and conversation, which can lead to constructive exchange between religious movements.[179] These comments are a bleak foreshadowing of the religious landscape years later, where models of interfaith dialogue must still confront the fundamentalism issues inherent in religion.

Knowing of the value of seeking interfaith dialogue, and recognising that the depth of genuine dialogue is often overlooked, Hunt elucidates the central aims of interfaith dialogue. She suggests that they are

> To grow in mutual understanding, respect, empathy and tolerance ... to break down barriers of suspicion and mistrust ... to expose and root out our own biases ... to foster harmony in our communities, and to advance collaboration in nurturing human flourishing at both local and global levels ... [and] to arrive at a deeper understanding of the other with whom we are in dialogue.[180]

Hunt stresses that the goal of interfaith exchange is not conversion, nor to weaken an individual's conviction of their own religious tradition, but to come to the point of genuine and mutual understanding.[181] This goal has been reinforced as the primary purpose of genuine interfaith dialogue as the concept has developed through history.

3.3 *A Brief History of Interfaith Dialogue*

Historically, interfaith dialogue has been initiated as a response to conflict, primarily because of exclusive truth claims between groups.[182] This notion of seeking truth has been a source of great tension in dialogue, but literature now seeks to ensure parties understand that truth is historical, intentional, perspectival, language-limited, interpretive, and dialogic.[183] If this perspective of truth is understood, dialogue is much more possible. Even though religious

178 Peter A. Huff, "The Challenge of Fundamentalism for Interreligious Dialogue," *Cross Currents* 50, no. 1/2 (2000): 94.

179 Ibid., 100.

180 Hunt, "Interfaith Dialogue: Lessons from the Ecumenical Movement," 9-10.

181 Ibid., 9-10.

182 Hames, "How Do Conflict Situations Affect Our Faith Communities and Our Interreligious Relationships?," 69.

183 Julia Sheetz-Willard et al., "Interreligious Dialogue Reconsidered: Learning from and Responding to Critique and Change," *Journal of Ecumenical Studies* 47, no. 2 (2012): 250.

groups may act toward each other in tolerance and cordiality, there is a deeper relationship that remains untapped due to the differences between groups.[184] At the beginning of interfaith dialogue's presence in scholarly analysis in 1962, the purpose of interfaith dialogue was promoted to not bring about religious unity, but to draw out the possibility of understanding and respect, where pluralism and coexistence can permeate the structures of society.[185] Though, Javier recognises that the processes of dialogue have developed significantly over time, he notes that early attempts at interfaith dialogue were initially formed around two factors, being (1) the theological evaluation of world religions, and (2) the meaning of the salvific plan inherent in these religious traditions.[186] These initial pursuits that informed initial interfaith dialogue have been reformed and refined over time.[187] While the practice of interfaith dialogue occurred much earlier, theologians and practitioners started building the scholarly base of literature in the 1960s with interfaith dialogue analysis accelerating in the late 1980s.[188] Contributions to the scholarship of interfaith dialogue remained limited to the scope of religious studies into the 1990s. However, the events of the new century brought new and sustained attention to interfaith dialogue from a variety of different specialties, including International Relations and Diplomacy Studies.[189]

Regarding the practice of interfaith dialogue, the World's Parliament of Religions, which took place in 1893, is generally considered as the major starting point.[190] Momentum accelerated when the 'Ecumenical Movement' started in 1910 to unify the Christian Church.[191] This was followed by a number of other initiatives, including the World Congress of Faiths in 1936, Religions for Peace in 1961, and the World Conference of Religions for Peace in 1970.[192] These conferences were organised summits for religious leaders to engage in dialogue, and from these major institutions other dialogue mechanisms developed. Since the reinvigoration of interfaith dialogue in response to 9/11, many other interfaith initiatives have emerged with a much broader geographical scope

184 Hames, "How Do Conflict Situations Affect Our Faith Communities and Our Interreligious Relationships?," 69.

185 J.E.W., "Interfaith Dialogue," *Journal of Church and State* 4, no. 1 (1962): 7.

186 Edgar Javier, "Interreligious Dialogue: Historical Constants and Challenges in Asia," *Philippiniana Sacra* 42, no. 125 (2007): 234.

187 For a timeline of the development of interfaith dialogue through this lens, see ibid., 234-244.

188 Neufeldt, "Interfaith Dialogue: Assessing Theories of Change," 347.

189 Ibid., 347.

190 Magonet, "The Growth of Interfaith Dialogue," 40.

191 Swidler, "Sorting out Meanings: 'Religion,' 'Spiritual,' 'Interreligious,' 'Interfaith,' Etc.," 379.

192 Magonet, "The Growth of Interfaith Dialogue," 40.

and membership than before.[193] There has also been a push from the Islamic community to engage in dialogue in a way that does not compromise Muslim objectives, with Muslim scholars working carefully to engage in the process while maintaining their own legitimacy in representing their communities and developing strategies for further dialogue in light of global events.[194] This constructively balances the Western dominance in the area.

Interfaith dialogue has been a predominantly Western and Christian experience, with interfaith dialogue being acknowledged within the Christian Church as a legitimate element of religious life with ecumenical cooperation and engagement being maintained as a prominent component of religious plurality within society.[195] Further entrenched in this perspective is the work of scholars in the field that highlight the biblical basis for interfaith relations, noting that missions and discipleship are appropriate modes for engaging in interfaith dialogue.[196] This was formalised in 1981 by the British Council of Churches who endorsed the Four Principles of Inter Faith Dialogue, being:

1. Dialogue begins when people meet each other;
2. Dialogue depends upon mutual understanding and mutual trust;
3. Dialogue makes it possible to share in service to the community;
4. Dialogue becomes the medium of authentic witness.[197]

While history may reflect a strong Christian perspective in this area, interfaith dialogue began incorporating Muslim states as participants in initiatives through the 1970s and 1980s, and increasingly in the 1990s Muslim states began embracing interfaith programs to even take the leadership role in their use.[198]

In terms of the interfaith dialogue between specific religious traditions, Ariel highlighted the significant waves of relations between Jewish and Christian communities over time. Early attempts at dialogue began in the late 19th century from liberal Protestants, which focused on cooperating on civic issues. Events were sporadic and generally only conducted out of personal friendship between leaders, but these channels were later reinforced through the World's Parliament of Religions.[199] This institution identified six concerns

193 See ibid., 41-2.

194 Argon, "Strategies for Interreligious and Inter-Muslim Dialogue: A Proposed Methodology," 363.

195 Douglas Pratt, "Christian Discipleship and Interfaith Engagement," *Pacifica* 22, no. 3 (2009): 317.

196 Ibid., 332.

197 Ibid., 317.

198 Kayaoglu, "Explaining Interfaith Dialogue in the Muslim World," 236.

199 Yaakov Ariel, "Interfaith Dialogue and the Golden Age of Christian-Jewish Relations" (2010): 1.

that it sought to address, but also formed the direction that future institutions could work toward. The six concerns include: (1) the struggle of 'interreligion' against the 'absence of religion' in modern secularism, (2) the need to overcome the historic connection between religious disagreement and violence, (3) religion as a liberating and motivating force for good in the world, (4) the significance of the Golden Rule as a potential focus for citizens in each country to help create and implement a global ethic, (5) the problematic of absolutism in commitment to a particular religious path versus the relativism of granting parity of value to all, and (6) the possibility of a mystical unity of the religions.[200] Through the 1950s and 1960s, international movements on interfaith dialogue had developed rapidly, including Christian ecumenical movements, the establishing of the World Council of Churches, and Nostra Aetate.[201] This time also encouraged the expansion of the scope of interfaith dialogue to include not only Jews and Christians. As a result of expanded dialogue initiatives, other participants were able to participate from the 1960s. These processes were called 'alternative interfaith dialogue,' developed to bring together Jewish communities with non-Jewish communities with the largest programs occurring in the United States and the United Kingdom.[202]

The Catholic-Jewish dialogue specifically has a strong history of engagement, including the Nostra Aetate statement discussed later. The long-term impacts built from this foundation still exists. In fact, in 2009, statements were made between Jewish and Catholic leaders that tasked each religious community with certain responsibilities to improve interfaith communities.[203] This agreement became known as the Twelve Points of Berlin which has four points of responsibility placed on the Christian community, four points on the Jewish community and also draws out four points for both communities to jointly pursue. These points highlight a formalised goal for interfaith dialogue, being:

1. To enhance interreligious and intercultural education;
2. To promote interreligious friendship and cooperation as well as social justice in the global society;
3. To enhance dialogue with political and economic bodies;
4. To network with all those whose work responds to the demands of environmental stewardship.[204]

---

200 Sheetz-Willard et al., "Interreligious Dialogue Reconsidered: Learning from and Responding to Critique and Change," 258.

201 Ariel, "Interfaith Dialogue and the Golden Age of Christian-Jewish Relations," 8.

202 Ibid., 16-17.

203 John T. Pawlikowski, "The State of the Global Catholic-Jewish Dialogue," *Studies in Christian-Jewish Relations* 5, no. 1 (2010): 2-3.

204 Ibid., 2-3.

These four points are a clear example of how interfaith dialogue can produce clear targets of mutual cooperation which guide the actions of differing religions toward positive global change.

Christian and Muslim relations also share in a rich history in interfaith engagement. Most of the relations go through periods of engagement and also conflict, but there are periods to draw upon to develop effective strategies. Khalidi sketches relations across four periods, being: (1) the age of triumph (7th-9th centuries), (2) the age of curiosity (10th-14th centuries), (3) the age of indifference (14th-17th centuries), and (4) the age of bafflement (18th-20th centuries).[205] Kerr observes that there is no single history of Christian-Muslim narratives, that the history of these relations are contextual and varied in experience, that the socio-political expression of the Christian-Muslim history is varied, and that Western European understandings of this relationship are seen as dominant only as a result of imperialism.[206] While these observations seem critical, they do demonstrate the difficult relations between the two religious groups, highlighting the importance of ensuring the best standard of interfaith dialogue in today's context.

Recognised through literature as a watershed in interfaith dialogue, between 1962 and 1965, the Second Vatican Council met to recommend directives to the Catholic Church globally, one of these being the implementation of interfaith dialogue.[207] In summary, the document acknowledges, "human connectedness is a reality that compels the Church to re-examine its relationship with other religions," thus, relationships should be re-contextualised to focus on common themes between religions and all of humanity.[208] While the Catholic Church was known to resist the ecumenical movement more broadly, this document not only promoted interfaith dialogue but also encouraged the 'Catholic faithful' to 'take the first steps' in initiating dialogue.[209] Since the publication of Nostra Aetate, the Catholic Church has pursued a consistent relationship between the world's major religions, and also promoted

205 John Borelli, "Christian-Muslim Relations in the United States: Reflections for the Future after Two Decades of Experience," *Muslim World* 94, no. 3 (2004): 331.

206 Ibid., 330.

207 See Pope Paul VI, "Declaration on the Relation of the Church to Non-Christian Religions: Nostra Aetate" http://www.vatican.va/archive/hist_councils/ii_vatican_council/documents/vat-ii_decl_19651028_nostra-aetate_en.html. Accessed on 14/11/2018.

208 SimonMary Asese Aihiokhai, "Going Beyond Nostra Aetate: The Way Forward for Interreligious Dialogue," *Journal of Ecumenical Studies* 51, no. 3 (2016): 387.

209 Leonard Swidler, "Sorting out Meanings: 'Religion,' 'Spiritual,' 'Interreligious,' 'Interfaith,' Etc.," ibid., 49 (2014): 379.

friendship with indigenous religions too.[210] The three enduring legacies of the Second Vatican Council are 'resourcement', that is the resourcing of theology in tradition, 'aggiornamento', or bringing the Church into the modern world, and 'conersazione', or dialogue and conversation with other religions.[211] In response to the position of the Catholic Church regarding interfaith dialogue, many Muslim groups began sharing open letters to their counterparts, calling for sincere and friendly relations between Christianity and Islam, highlighting that at the root of their religions is the Abrahamic traditions and the commandments of love.[212]

Some criticisms were given to Nostra Aetate because it suggested that religion is solely a positive experience and disregarded the way in which religion had been distorted and used to commit violence throughout history.[213] This means that although the doors were opened for interfaith dialogue, criticality must still be applied to external and internal aspect of religious relations. While some recognised the broad set of changes encouraged by Nostra Aetate, some were unhappy with the liturgical changes and the way that the process seemed to veer from magisterial traditions.[214] These criticisms have been managed over time, but the Second Vatican Council did mark a shift in the exploration of interfaith programs.

The Vatican continued to build on this body of work by putting forward four types of dialogue as outlined in the 1984 Dialogue and Mission and 1991 Dialogue and Proclamation documents. They outline dialogue, summarised by Manion, as:

1. The dialogue of life, where people strive to live in an open and neighbourly spirit, sharing their joys and sorrows, their human problems and preoccupations;
2. The dialogue of action, in which Christians and others collaborate for the integral development and liberation of people;
3. The dialogue of theological exchange, where specialists seek to deepen their understanding of their respective religious heritages, and to appreciate each other's spiritual views; and,

210 SimonMary Asese Aihiokhai, "Going Beyond Nostra Aetate: The Way Forward for Interreligious Dialogue," ibid., 51 (2016): 386.

211 Maria Massi Dakake, "A Good Word Is as a Good Tree: A Muslim Response to the Interfaith Challenges of Vatican II," *Modern Theology* 29, no. 4 (2013): 189.

212 "Muslim Proposal Towards a Common Base of Interreligious Dialogue," *Advocatus* 14, no. 28 (2017): 2.

213 Baum, "Interreligious Dialogue Includes Listening to Secular Voices," 365.

214 Dakake, "A Good Word Is as a Good Tree: A Muslim Response to the Interfaith Challenges of Vatican II," 189.

4. The dialogue of religious experience, where persons, rooted in their own religious traditions, share their spiritual riches, for instance with regard to prayer and contemplation, faith and ways of searching for God or the Absolute.[215]

Many scholars have used these categorisations of dialogue as they give a framework for the multiple levels of exchange that can take place in dialogue.

The Christian religious perspective was not the only one to engage in this type of declaration for interfaith engagement. With respect to the Christian-Muslim interfaith engagement, a Muslim statement called 'A Common Word Between Us and You' was released in 2007 and became a focal point of discussion between Christian and Muslim leaders.[216] This was penned as an open letter written by Muslim scholars and leaders to be received by Pope Benedict XVI and Christian authorities. The document appeals to the common belief in the love of God and the love of one's neighbour, using Quranic texts to validate these claims. It concludes by calling for Christians to "come together with us on the common essentials of our two religions."[217] While the Christian response to this document has been mixed, but in terms of the wider phenomenon of interfaith dialogue, formal statements of this nature aid in bringing together groups to lively debate which does, at the very least, begin in building pathways for genuine relationships to be built.[218] Even though these statements can be inspiring and provide some frameworks for practical dialogue, there are some areas that still can be improved. Ali recommends, (1) understanding that the rules for having any sort of conversation and dialogue across religious and cultural lines are not very different from the rules that one needs to stick to for having successful interpersonal relationships, (2) understanding the worldviews of the participants of the dialogue, and (3) disentangling the issue of salvation from the dialogue.[219] These are specific recommendations coming from the exchange mentioned above, but they do highlight the areas where major religious statements can be strengthened to support the broader work of interfaith dialogue.

---

215 Gerard Mannion, "Pathways for Dialogue in the 21st Century: What We Learned at Assisi 2012" (2013): 393.

216 Gordon Nickel, "The Use of Sūra 3:64 in Interfaith Appeals: Dialogue or Da'wa?," (Paternoster Periodicals, 2016), 346.

217 Ibid., 346.

218 Ibid., 355.

219 Muhammad Modassir Ali, "A Muslim Interfaith Initiative (a Common Word between Us and You) and Its Christian Response," *Insights* 2, no. 1 (2009): 121.

3.4 *Preconditions to Interfaith Dialogue*

There are several preconditions that should be satisfied to ensure the most successful dialogue. A key lesson learnt from the historical examples of interfaith dialogue, as proffered by Magonet, is that "religions do not meet: people meet."[220] This point seeks to reorient the perspective of participants in interfaith dialogue, noting that it is not religions that are engaging in dialogue but individuals who identify with a specific religious tradition. Early encounters of interfaith dialogue were often difficult because individuals were met with prejudices and tension by virtue of ongoing conflict between religious traditions, which then reinforced the image of this person as 'the other'.[221] Jütte supports this claim, noting that when early interfaith encounters began between Christian and Jewish groups, parties were seen as 'Jew' and 'Christian', rather than as "individuals embedded in a multifaceted reality."[222] When dialogue is approached on a more personal basis, regarding participants as individuals, the dialogue is more fruitful and engaging for the parties involved. This also serves to ensure that no party is neglected or marginalised in the discussion.

From this basis, before even considering the practical model of interfaith dialogue, Orton provides a list of seven key questions that should be answered to help frame the most effective process of interfaith dialogue. They are:

1. Who is involved?
2. Who is missing?
3. What is the dialogue for?
4. How is the complexity of diversity understood to affect interfaith dialogue?
5. What conditions enable effective interfaith dialogue?
6. How are the dynamics of participation and representation by different individuals and groups handled?
7. What dilemmas may arise within interfaith dialogue, and how might these be handled by those involved?[223]

These guiding questions are valuable as they set a healthy foundation to mitigate any potential problems that may arise before interfaith dialogue begins. These questions may also clarify which model of dialogue will be best suited for the issue that needs to be addressed. This is why Orton notes that there is no one-size-fits-all approach to interfaith dialogue, but rather promotes the

220 Magonet, "The Growth of Interfaith Dialogue," 39-40.

221 Ibid., 39-40.

222 Daniel Jütte, "Interfaith Encounters between Jews and Christians in the Early Modern Period and Beyond: Toward a Framework", *The American Historical Review*, 118 (2013): 382.

223 Orton, "Interfaith Dialogue: Seven Key Questions for Theory, Policy and Practice," 353-361.

need to recognise dialogue at multiple levels.[224] Mandour also suggests some other central principles that should be sought in order to build trust and set a positive foundation for dialogue. These are recognition, a basis of equality between individuals, mutual respect between participants, dialogue between at least two parties, a pursuit of tolerance, and an overarching process of joint cooperation.[225] In a similar way, Leggewie promotes the 'Ten Commandments to Interfaith Dialogue' which form guiding principles when considering the structures and framing of interfaith dialogues. These commandments include never forcing parties into dialogue, avoiding lazy peace agreements, not focusing on God exclusively, avoiding political correctness, and examining personal actions, among others.[226] This again highlights the importance placed on preparing the groundwork if interfaith dialogue is to be successful.

To set the best foundation for interfaith dialogue, comprehensive studies conclude that the primary requisite for positive dialogue is humility, particularly in the area of doctrine.[227] This is a challenge because typically believers of religions attribute the blame for conflict to their counterparts, and thus humility requires participants to understand that they may have contributed to the issues more than they have to the solutions.[228] In later writings, Burrell still recommends humility as the foundation for interfaith dialogue, but also urges parties to frame interfaith dialogue as a way to learn from each other, recognising the mutual need for contributions from all participants.[229] Others identify two temptations that participants must overcome before entering into dialogue. These are that participants maintain their beliefs are the sole true beliefs, suggesting that other beliefs are false, or maintaining that their beliefs are the sole completely true beliefs, suggesting that other beliefs are either distorted or incomplete.[230] Being wary of humility and truth claims are helpful to ensure that participants do not engage in dialogue with preconceptions that may hinder genuine exchange.

---

224 Ibid., 360.

225 Mandour, "Islam and Religious Freedom: Role of Interfaith Dialogue in Promoting Global Peace," 888-889.

226 These commandments are explored fully in Claus Leggewie, "Dialogue? Thank You, No! Ten Commandments for Interfaith Dialogue," *European Judaism* 37, no. 1 (2004).

227 David B. Burrell, "Some Requisites for Interfaith Dialogue," *New Blackfriars* 89, no. 1021 (2008): 310.

228 Ibid., 301.

229 "Christian-Muslim Dialogue in a World Gone Religiously Awry," *Muslim World* 100, no. 4 (2010): 423.

230 W. T. Dickens, "Frank Conversations: Promoting Peace among the Abrahamic Traditions through Interreligious Dialogue," (Wiley-Blackwell, 2006), 398.

Building on these ideas, Tyagananda proposes several conditions that are pertinent to successful dialogue. The first is that the participants accept there is a possibility of learning something new in the exchange. There must not be an expectation of merely giving a single perspective, but there should be an exchange in place where the participants are willing to learn. An extension to this is the need for parties to listen. They must listen and respect participants to minimise biases and prejudices. The next condition is to avoid making any assumptions. This often means not coming to the discussion with explicit agendas and every topic should be negotiable. The next condition is that dialogue partners must be willing to discuss not just common themes, but they must not shy away from exploring differences, as that is what will help illuminate true understanding of ideas, symbols, words and rituals.[231] Much like in diplomacy, those seeking to initiate interfaith dialogue must be mindful of the preconditions going into dialogue, ensuring that the context is adequately set to achieve as much success as possible.

3.5 *Models of Interfaith Dialogue*

With the foundations of interfaith dialogue considered, the most appropriate method of dialogue must be employed to have the best chances of achieving the desired outcome. The following paragraphs propose a variety of different interfaith models that have been discussed in the literature. This is by no means an exhaustive review of the literature on the topic, but it does provide a variety of different forms and examples to give an understanding of some methods available. In general, Shoemaker and Edmonds suggest that interfaith movements are "constitutive of dialogue and service opportunities, and importantly, … have strict rules against proselytism."[232] In a basic form of dialogue, one religious group will present information about their faith discuss subjective elements of religiosity.[233] There are a variety of interfaith dialogues with varying degrees of complexity. Simple forms of interfaith dialogue can operate at a low level. For example, there are examples of dialogues based around meals where spaces are created to allow participants to engage in dialogue, following the World Café Dialogue or the Let's Talk Lunch Dialogues approach.[234] The purpose of these groups is to allow communities, in this case

---

231 Swami Tyagananda, "Doing Dialogue Interreligiously," *Dialog: A Journal of Theology* 50, no. 3 (2011): 229.

232 Shoemaker and Edmonds, "The Limits of Interfaith? Interfaith Identities, Emerging Potentialities, and Exclusivity," 201.

233 Ibid., 201.

234 Holland and Walker, "Choice Theory and Interfaith Dialogue: Building Relationships between Faiths and Embracing Diversity," 19.

students, to begin conversations and start forming interfaith relationships. Beyond this, however, numerous different models of interfaith engagement have been developed, for example Khan's study of neighbourhood, institutional, scriptural, campaigning, pastoral and women's interfaith initiatives.[235] The models are diverse, using numerous different groups and forms to target different audiences and achieve various results. They have developed even to include using 'Transformative Music Communication' as a way to create spaces for transformative communication that engage in the dynamics of culture and identity in a peaceful way.[236] The variety of models suggests several opportunities that could be integrated into diplomatic strategy depending on what goals have been set.

For a comprehensive and organised structure for interfaith dialogue, McCormack provides a multilevel model for the social dimensions of interfaith relations.[237] There are three levels to this model. The first is the macrosystemic, which focuses on socio-historical trends, theological systems, and the institutional element of religion. The second level is the mesosystemic level, which looks at religious organisations, places of worship and religious coalitions. The third level is the microsystemic, which examines individual religious behaviours and interpersonal contact.[238] This model recognises the social impact of religion and identifies the different levels of society that religion manifests. Clarifying these levels is helpful when identifying the best possible implementation of interfaith dialogue.

A prolific writer in the space of interfaith dialogue is Paul Knitter and many academics have tested his proposed models for dialogue. There are four prominent models for dialogue that Knitter offers when determining how a religious group perceived their own beliefs. This is important as it can be a good indicator as to the type of dialogue required between groups. They are:

1. The replacement model, which remains exclusivist about which is the true religion and does not yet engage in dialogue.
2. The fulfilment model, which sees participants believe in God's love but note that salvation can only come in one particular religion, and therefore does not validate any value or truth claim made within other religions.

---

235 Humera Khan, "Interfaith Contributions to a Just Society," *European Judaism* 48, no. 2 (2015): 47.

236 King, "Music, Peacebuilding, and Interfaith Dialogue: Transformative Bridges in Muslim–Christian Relations," 204.

237 McCormack, "Interfaith Relations in the United States: Toward a Multilevel Community Psychology Approach," 176.

238 Ibid., 176.

3. The mutuality model, where followers believe that there are many true religions and that dialogue between those religions becomes imperative. This model sees equality between religions in that each participant has the right to speak and be heard.
4. The acceptance model, which builds on the mutuality model in that there is an acceptance that there is no real common ground between religions, and therefore it is impossible for one religion to fully understand another. Here, religious groups must protect the real differences between religious traditions.[239]

These perspectives can suggest the willingness of religious groups to engage in dialogue. Furthermore, they are reflected in broad dialogical attitudes, being exclusivism, inclusivism, parallelism and pluralism. Zia-ul-Haq summarises each of these attitudes, stating:

> Exclusivists participate in dialogue to show that they hold their faith as the only true path of salvation. Inclusivists recognise the possibility of truth in others, but they consider them not so corrupted as they recognise that others' faith can be included in their own, that their faith tradition is more comprehensive or universal and thus has room to 'include' the faith of the other. Parallelists allow other faiths to run parallel without interference. The most suitable attitude for dialogue is pluralism, which aims at proper understanding and searches for common grounds of co-operation and coexistence. Except the diehard fanatics who would like to convert all to their doctrine, it is apparent to everyone that religious pluralism is a fact of today's world.[240]

The four models and dialogic attitudes overlap, as explored by Tyagananda. Exclusivists support the replacement model, as the goal of religion becomes replacing false teaching. The inclusivist attitude is applied to the fulfilment model. Elements of the parallel and pluralist attitudes then come into play when exploring the mutuality and acceptance model. Here, pluralism is again promoted as the ideal attitude to have toward dialogue as it sees diversity of religious traditions not as a problem, but as an opportunity for expanded social cohesion, cooperation and understanding.[241] Understanding the attitude and

239 Lyn Parker, "Religious Education for Peaceful Coexistence in Indonesia?," *South East Asia Research* 22, no. 4 (2014): 493.

240 Muhammad Zia-ul-Haq, "Muslims' Participation in Interfaith Dialogue: Challenges and Prospects," (University of Pennsylvania Press, 2014), 617.

241 Tyagananda, "Doing Dialogue Interreligiously," 228.

perspective of interlocutors as they approach interfaith dialogue helps clarify the goals, intents and potential behaviours of groups before they enter into dialogue. This will also provide strategies with confidence in the method of dialogue they choose to apply between the groups, potentially enhancing the probability of successful dialogue.

Knitters' theory of 'liberative dialogue' forms the basis of one method of interfaith dialogue. In this model, dialogue starts from non-religious issues, perhaps on focusing initially on a problem in the community like conflict, and then moves through four steps, being: compassion, conversion, collaboration, and comprehension.[242] The compassion stage draws out shared feelings and highlights the common humanity of the groups, and then in the conversion stage, participants can change their perspectives after recognising the suffering of the other parties.[243] Here, conversion does not refer to proselytization, but rather converting thinking toward a certain group. The third stage, collaboration, sees members working together to address the suffering of the groups which leads to the fourth stage, comprehension, where genuine interfaith dialogue begins between participants as they comprehend the texts and values that have led individuals to these behaviours.[244]

Christian Siregar explores some of Knitter's other models for dialogue, which were tested in Indonesia. This model moved through three stages of dialogue. First, there should be a focus in terms of the specific theme being addressed in dialogue. Second, there is a multilevel dialogue performed in the process, recognising that not every form of dialogue is suitable for every context. Finally, the action taken place at the conclusion of the dialogue should be narrowed to focus on improving living standards. This model engages at the community level and helps improve structural issues that aid in alleviating conflict, but also are in line with the missional teachings of religions.[245] This model highlights the need for a targeted approach to dialogue and, when tested in Indonesia, found success in addressing communal issues following conflict.

Neufeldt promotes another approach to interfaith dialogue and finds that there are three basic orientations with respect to how genuine change can emerge through dialogue. These orientations are theological, political and peacebuilding. These approaches are framed by assumptions in the scholarship of these perspectives. The theological viewpoint is developed from

242 Muwahidah, "Interfaith Dialogue at the Grassroots Level: A Case Study of an Interfaith Empowerment Program in East Java, Indonesia," 86.

243 Ibid., 86.

244 Ibid., 86.

245 Siregar Christian, "Pluralism and Religious Tolerance in Indonesia: An Ethical-Theological Review Based on Christian Faith Perspectives," *Humaniora* 7, no. 3 (2016): 355-356.

religious studies, political science and international relations inform the political model, and peacebuilding and conflict transformation scholarship informs the peacebuilding approach. These respective areas "demonstrate divergent views of the intersection of politics, religion, and conflict and generate very different formats as well as expectations and outcomes" regarding the role and influence of interfaith dialogue.[246] Neufeldt's approaches to interfaith dialogue are helpful in identifying the root causes of conflict leading to dialogue and can be useful in supporting diplomatic programs.

Noting that dialogue should not only be built around what is common between religions, the four broad types of dialogue – dialogue of life, of action, of theological exchange, and of religious experience – must be applied also to cases of similarity but used as an opportunity to clarify differences.[247] These broad strategies have been applied and adapted by other scholars. Bakker suggests that the literature predominantly focuses on three types of dialogue, being:

1. The dialogue of life, taking place where people of various religious backgrounds live together and meet one another.
2. The dialogue of the mind, organised between scholars and religious experts.
3. The dialogue of the heart, occurring between monastics, mystics and other people with an antenna for mysticism.

While these concepts do overlap, and other scholars choose to use different terms for these approaches, they provide an insight into the various levels dialogue can be promoted.

Another prominent scholar in this field, Leonard Swidler, has worked to define the key features and modes of interfaith dialogue, famously proposing ten principles for interfaith dialogue. These principles have been strengthened through academic studies and provide a guideline for engaging in interfaith dialogue. The ten principles for dialogue are:

1. Be willing to learn, to grow, and to participate in change.
2. Dialogue is needed both among differing groups and within the same group.
3. Practice honesty and sincerity.
4. Start dialogue with points where agreement is easier.
5. Compare and contrast similar elements of differing traditions.

246 Neufeldt, "Interfaith Dialogue: Assessing Theories of Change," 347. To see how these different perspectives are broken down, see ibid., 348.

247 Aihiokhai, "Going Beyond Nostra Aetate: The Way Forward for Interreligious Dialogue," 398.

6. Identify oneself so that someone could speak for you with understanding.
7. Learn how to listen with an open mind without projecting oneself into what 'the other' is saying.
8. Level the playing field; as far as possible counter unequal power relations.
9. Risk self-critical thinking on behalf of increasing knowledge.
10. Practice empathy.[248]

From Swidler's experience, integrating these into the interfaith process will promote a more genuine and more efficacious dialogue.

Noting that a central starting point of interfaith dialogue is to highlight the common humanity between religious groups, Swidler proposes 'The Dialogues of Humanity' which are built around four dimensions. These are:

1. The cognitive or intellectual. This relates to truth-seeking, also referred to as the dialogue of the head, where participants engage with the intellectual questions of religion and identity. This approach relies on an epistemological paradigm, meaning that participants will seek 'understanding of how we humans understand.'
2. The illative or ethical. Swidler refers to this as seeking the good, or the dialogue of the hands. Interfaith participants, through this approach, are encouraged to work together to build a better community to live in. As it is a shared community, groups must work jointly to achieve these goals. This approach focuses on bringing healing to groups and dismantling the concept of the 'other' within society.
3. The affective, aesthetic/spiritual. This relates to seeking the spiritual, referred to as the dialogue of the heart. It exposes individuals to the beauty of the other noting the bodily-spiritual expression and responses to life. Here, music, dance, poetry are noted as expressions of the heart, and they expose a deeper, more spiritual dimension to humanity that can be engaged with through dialogue.
4. Holiness, or 'seeking the One.' This approach pursues a holistic life that, in religious terms, encourages participants to work toward holiness. This is a reflective dialogue that requires self-examination to build holiness in the individual, and allow that to impact the broader group.[249]

Some scholars have worked with Swidler's models and adapted them in light of the advancements in the field. This includes Swidler's 'Stages of Transformation' which focuses on the practices embedded in the human condition

248 Julia Sheetz-Willard et al., "Interreligious Dialogue Reconsidered: Learning from and Responding to Critique and Change," ibid., 47, no. 2 (2012): 259-260.

249 Leonard Swidler, "Sorting out Meanings: 'Religion,' 'Spiritual,' 'Interreligious,' 'Interfaith,' Etc.," ibid., 49, no. 3 (2014): 377-378.

that inform an individual's beliefs to encourage them to act toward a global ethic. The first practice is called encountering, which focuses on recognising differences that create 'the other' and generate conflict and fear. The next is making a conscious choice to engage with one another and not withdraw or fight. The next is passing over, which means expressing interest and empathy in dialogue. Active relationships are the next practice, where a continuation of encounters between each group is set into place. Next, dialogic awakening refers to moments of genuine empathy and understanding that emerge from dialogue. This leads to a humanitarian 'global awaking,' which means critical thinking is applied to find solutions toward the common good. The final practice is building moral consciousness, ensuring that practices in the future are born of empathy and critical thinking.[250] This development of the dialogue process illustrates how dialogue can transform relationships and lead to a common purpose within society, but also demonstrates that advancements in the study of interfaith dialogue are refining models, giving justification to the potential of incorporating diplomacy into an interfaith approach.

Dickens proposes a model of dialogue that finds its roots in philosophical thought. Here, the model of dialogue provided by Socrates and Plato encourages participants to seek mutual understanding by pursuing truth through enquiry.[251] While participants believe that they are in line with truth, they recognise that they could be wrong and are open to pursuing truth with the broader group. The challenges with applying this process to interfaith dialogue are that it assumes that truth is already known but has been forgotten, or it implies a power imbalance where one participant drives the questions of inquiry and potentially dictate the outcomes of the dialogue.[252] Dickens provides another model that reframes dialogue to be viewed as a gathering of siblings. Here, whether participants are friendly with each other or not, they are bound together by a deeper connection – namely, love.[253] Upon reviewing multiple models for interfaith dialogue, Dickens proposes a virtue-based approach to dialogue that integrates the virtues prominent within Abrahamic tradition – honesty, empathy, and humility – and utilises these virtues as a motivator for dialogue and positive action between religious groups.[254]

250 Julia Sheetz-Willard et al., "Interreligious Dialogue Reconsidered: Learning from and Responding to Critique and Change," ibid., 47, no. 2 (2012): 268.

251 Dickens, "Frank Conversations: Promoting Peace among the Abrahamic Traditions through Interreligious Dialogue," 409-411.

252 Ibid., 409-411.

253 Ibid., 411.

254 Ibid., 413.

As these virtues are derived from religious texts and traditions, using these assets to underpin the dialogue process is another model that has gained support from observers. Practical approaches to dialogue may include interreligious hermeneutics and scriptural studies. Hermeneutics looks to theories and methods of interpretation and understanding which can move beyond traditional religious boundaries, and scriptural analysis is a specific extension of this process.[255] This has been developed into a method of interfaith dialogue called religious readings. Here groups come together and share religious texts, engaging in debate about the scriptures, their meaning, and perhaps even the commonalities shared between different religious traditions. While this approach to interfaith dialogue is not new, the history of scriptural reading often repeats the same conclusion in that participants stall dialogue on the theme and content of the scripture, and rather rebut the authenticity of the other's religious texts.[256] Some prefer to call this process comparative theological readings, where participants write on theology from a context that has been developed from insights revealed from other perspectives.

The aim of scriptural reading is informed by the context of the dialogue, that is, the central issues that are trying to be addressed and creating a structure that will see that manifested through dialogue.[257] Typically this means that parties are using religious scripture as a way to enhance understanding and knowledge of other beliefs which allows participants to not only share from their own experiences, but have their own beliefs reflectively understood as well.[258] Conceptually, religious reading exercises familiarise groups with different religious contexts, which reveal how interpretations are made within these texts, and then those texts are reinterpreted through the lens of the processes described by the other parties. This process of learning how to interpret scripture through other methods is known as recontextualization.[259] This type of approach is beneficial to inspiring dialogue as "there is no established, approved set of margins within which the reading can be contained; nor is there any entirely adequate summation, before or after the reading,

255 Kari Storstein Haug, "Possibilities and Limitations of Interreligious Scripture Reading," *Mission Studies: Journal of the International Association for Mission Studies* 31, no. 2 (2014): 158.

256 A. Rashied Omar, "Embracing the "Other" as an Extension of the Self: Muslim Reflections on the Epistle to the Hebrews 13:2," *Anglican Theological Review* 91, no. 3 (2009): 433.

257 Haug, "Possibilities and Limitations of Interreligious Scripture Reading," 159.

258 Ibid., 159.

259 Tracy Sayuki Tiemeier, "Interreligious Reading in the Context of Dialogue: When Interreligious Reading 'Fails'," *Modern Theology* 29, no. 4 (2013): 147-148.

of what the juxtaposition is supposed to mean."[260] Like other models of interfaith dialogue, this process allows for genuine impact as a result of mutual exchange.

One point to consider when engaging in religious reading is the importance of language and clarifying that language so that interfaith dialogue is not built on ambiguities or skewed perceptions of the text.[261] As is common in religious tradition, language can take literal and symbolic forms, which means that participants can sometimes bias their language preferences based on concepts which may disempower other participants.[262] Omar offers the example of holding a dialogue in English in a region where less proficient English speakers are required to engage in dialogue about scripture, noting that this inherently will limit the outcomes of the process. Religious reading helps to achieve something that is often missed in general interfaith dialogue. For transparent and effectual dialogue to occur, it is imperative that not only commonalities are recognised, but understanding the differences between traditions and theologies assists in results in genuine dialogue.[263] This phenomenon in a dialogue process is called translation. Here, in dialogue, the participant must understand their own beliefs and teachings before then expressing and exchanging them with their dialogue partner.[264] Using the correct language and examining the differences of beliefs revealed through dialogue can see scriptural reading as a basis for further dialogic exchange.

Scripture reading, in this context, is contemplative and ruminative and focuses on the quality of depth, not the amount of text covered.[265] It allows participants to linger on scripture for a longer period of time to avoid obvious and superficial interpretations but also encourages the dialogue to not move away from problematic passages in scripture to allow the uncomfortable elements of theology better understood by all parties.[266] This is a benefit of scriptural exchange in that it allows a framework that moves across religious boundaries, where separate groups have a guide for discussion.[267] This can be complementary to comparative theology as it allows groups to listen and

260 Ibid., 147-148.
261 "Muslim Proposal Towards a Common Base of Interreligious Dialogue," 9.
262 Omar, "Embracing the "Other" as an Extension of the Self: Muslim Reflections on the Epistle to the Hebrews 13:2," 434.
263 "Muslim Proposal Towards a Common Base of Interreligious Dialogue," 9.
264 Haug, "Possibilities and Limitations of Interreligious Scripture Reading," 165.
265 Dakake, "A Good Word Is as a Good Tree: A Muslim Response to the Interfaith Challenges of Vatican II," 192.
266 Ibid., 192.
267 Haug, "Possibilities and Limitations of Interreligious Scripture Reading," 166.

engage with the interpretation of scriptures from a variety of perspectives.[268] Haug notes that the main benefits of religious reading as a form of dialogue is that it can deepen understanding between participants, it gives a gives a concrete form to the discussion, it can open up dialogue to key questions and concerns, and deepen the friendship between groups to then allow discussion to develop to other areas pertinent to interfaith dialogue.[269] This is why it is a common approach to interfaith dialogue as it provides a natural agenda and form to the meeting. To improve scripture reading in the future, Omar encourages observers to recognise interpretative ambivalence, construct coherent ways to deal with texts, symbols and rituals that display ambivalence, and base arguments on religious texts and stories that lead toward healing, not conflict, to draw out the highest chance of transformation.[270] Being mindful of these recommendations will ensure that future programs incorporating religious reading will have more success as part of a broader dialogue strategy.

Incorporating the complementary trends in contemporary reconciliation theory as a framework for achieving pluralistic inclusivism in society through dialogue is another model that has been proposed.[271] Observers note that reconciliation is a powerful motivator at the heart of dialogue that guides participants beyond polite exchange and brings groups toward peacebuilding processes.[272] Incorporating restorative justice considerations can strengthen this approach. The concepts of restorative justice have been helpful in conflict resolution techniques, including in developing truth-telling, reconciliation and justice commissions at the community level.[273] These are all concepts that have transformed conflict resolution approaches and are inherent as goals of dialogue, and so this complementarity can be strengthened through formalised mechanisms. Recognising reconciliation as a process of repairing relationship between parties will enhance the dialogue process between religious groups and work toward establishing peace and justice within the community.[274]

268 Ibid., 166.

269 Ibid., 168-169.

270 Omar, "Embracing the 'Other' as an Extension of the Self: Muslim Reflections on the Epistle to the Hebrews 13:2," 437.

271 Todd Johanson, "Pluralistic Inclusivism and Christian-Muslim Dialogue: The Challenge of Moving Beyond Polite Discussion toward Reconciliation and Peace," *Journal of Ecumenical Studies* 51, no. 1 (2016): 47.

272 Ibid., 47.

273 Ibid., 48.

274 Ibid., 53.

3.6 *Interfaith Dialogue from an Islamic Perspective*

As interfaith dialogue has been developed from a predominantly Christian, Western perspective, scholars and practitioners have begun correcting this imbalance by investigating the methods of interfaith dialogue from the Islamic perspective. In general, dialogue can be drawn as a positive aspect in Islamic teachings as it develops understanding and cooperation.[275] In fact, as one of the major world religions based on Abrahamic roots, the Islamic doctrine of dialogue between faiths recognises that there is the basis of truth in other religions.[276] As a result of this shared foundation, there are many avenues where dialogue from the Islamic perspective can naturally occur.

A strategy that has been promoted for fruitful interfaith dialogue from the Muslim perspective focuses on utilising small groups for dialogue. These groups work toward a clear goal that seeks to maintain common traditional Islamic ideologies with outcomes testable by classical Islamic criteria.[277] Basing the methodology of interfaith dialogue on traditional Islamic constructs allows groups, particularly Muslim minorities, to accredit some authenticity and credibility to the interfaith process, resulting in deeper engagement.[278] A specific methodology that has been used to frame this approach is Gilmore's method for formulating strategy in dialogue. The six steps Gilmore proposes are to:

1. Record current strategy;
2. Identify problems;
3. Discover the core elements;
4. Formulate alternatives;
5. Evaluate alternatives;
6. Choose new strategy.[279]

Argon notes that this six-step process is able to guide the small groups through the dialogue processes to ensure that the ultimate goals of dialogue are achieved. This model focuses on the method and process of dialogue and gives space to adjust accordingly, but has been seen to work within Muslim communities.

Hermansen suggests the performative model of interfaith dialogue as a workable model within the Muslim experience. Conversational dialogues are structured around discussing shared issues over an extended period of time to build trust and relations with more substantial issues like doctrinal

---

275 Zia-ul-Haq, "Muslims' Participation in Interfaith Dialogue: Challenges and Prospects," 617.
276 Ibid., 618.
277 Argon, "Strategies for Interreligious and Inter-Muslim Dialogue: A Proposed Methodology," 356.
278 Ibid., 356.
279 Ibid., 358.

debate then finding its way on the agenda.[280] This type of approach takes time to build relationships between participants and may just circulate didactic, apologetic concepts without necessarily progressing in terms of achieving the goals of interfaith dialogue. The performative model seeks to legitimise the actors in the dialogue by focusing on the authority and ability to perform religious duties.[281] For example, Muslim roles will often be discussed in terms of who has the authority to represent Islam, who can correct the misinterpretations of the Islamic tradition, who can lead the discussions and so on. Instead of just meeting for the sake of conversation, Hermansen notes that Muslims performing interfaith dialogue helps highlight claims to authority, ritual and convention.[282] This builds on the work of Islamic scholars who have studied how mosques and places of worship, prayer, texts and rituals can be upheld and recognised through interfaith dialogue.[283] Approaching dialogue in this way better fits the values in the Islamic tradition.

One motivation for Muslim communities to participate in interfaith dialogue is to "[propagate] Islam, [provide] clear understanding about its tenets and sometimes for the sake of securing their interests in countries where they live in as minorities."[284] Mitwally Ibrahimi examines the Muslim perspective of interfaith dialogue through a legal lens noting that using Islamic legal content, such as Da'wah, to validate the Islamic contribution that could be made in interfaith dialogue strengthens their commitment to the process.[285] Other perspectives are also offered, including recommending international humanitarian cooperation and dialogue related to issues such as human rights, war, hunger, environmental relief efforts and so on, where the global challenges can bring participants together to address social justice and community issues which the Islamic voice is required to speak on.[286] In a contemporary setting, Islamic scholars favour Muslim participation in interfaith dialogue as true humanity, dignity and justice can only be achieved through cooperation, and that these exchanges can genuinely build understanding namely with the 'people of the book,' which results in compassion to all living beings.[287]

280 Marcia Hermansen, "Muslims in the Performative Mode: A Reflection on Muslim-Christian Dialogue," *Muslim World* 94, no. 3 (2004): 389.

281 Ibid., 390.

282 Ibid., 390.

283 Mohammad Said Mitwally Ibrahim, "Interfaith Dialogue a Muslim Legal Perspective on Its Validity, Concept and Practices," *Insights* 3, no. 1 (2010): 125-126.

284 Ibid., 94.

285 Ibid., 95-96.

286 Ibid., 110.

287 Zia-ul-Haq, "Muslims' Participation in Interfaith Dialogue: Challenges and Prospects," 633.

Achieving this broader engagement does still require a level of backing from Islamic theology to strengthen wide-base support. Khan reflected on Islamic theology to identify Islamic principles that could motivate successful interfaith engagement. Drawing on concepts from the Hadith and Quran, Khan puts forward four central tasks for engaging in dialogue, being: clarifying intentions, building relationships, working toward a common good, and working together for shared concerns.[288] Generally Muslim actors are motivated by two factors when engaging in interfaith strategies. The first is the idea of political theology – where religious actors express their perspectives on justice and political legitimacy – which has been based on religious texts and interpretations to inform their engagement with political structures.[289] The second factor highlights institutional relationships, here focusing on how religious actors and political authorities engage with one another.[290] Understanding these two factors can help recognise the influence of religious actors on democratisation, peacebuilding, conflict and even terrorism.[291] Kayaoglu finds that two factors have contributed to strategies used at a variety of levels within the community, including at the state level, which has a direct impact on diplomatic policies.[292] Mahmood takes a similar approach and applies interfaith dialogue to Muslim youth in the United Kingdom, finding that dialogue has curbed those who appear vulnerable to extremist ideologies, particularly in the prison system.[293] The methodology applied in this context has three parts: (1) a theological-theoretical aspect which shares religious texts to invalidate extremist doctrine and legitimise the interfaith process, (2) an educational aspect which teaches participants how to best interpret religious texts to avoid manipulation in the future, and (3) an empirical aspect which uses data collection and analysis to measure the impact of teachings and substantiate the results of the dialogue process.[294] Using Islamic theology as a basis for building support for interfaith processes has seen Muslim communities become more willing to participate to achieve goals and even influence state policies.

Another area that has found some success in building an Islamic base for interfaith dialogue is by developing interreligious education. In fact, Pallavicini highlights this as an area of strong potential from the Islamic perspective.

288 Khan, "Interfaith Contributions to a Just Society," 52-53.

289 Kayaoglu, "Explaining Interfaith Dialogue in the Muslim World," 237-238.

290 Ibid., 237-238.

291 Ibid., 237-238.

292 See ibid., 238-239.

293 Tariq Mahmood, "Interfaith Dialogue and British Muslim Prisoners," (University of Pennsylvania Press, 2016), 598-599.

294 Ibid., 598-599.

Education can be a vehicle to enhance relationships between Muslim communities and other communities in the world where they are marginalised and facing social tension.[295] In developing educational strategies, interreligious education must be distinct from monoreligious education and multi-religious education. The latter places importance on diversity by studying objective descriptions and doctrinal specifications. Interfaith education looks at the deeper principles of identity and culture, dialogue, cooperation and the development of relationships.[296] It is this approach that will translate best to effective diplomatic strategies and conflict resolution, assist in preventing radicalism and protect minorities from persecution.[297]

Scholars involved in dialogue have proposed frameworks that specifically address the potential hesitance that Muslim people may have toward engaging in interfaith dialogue. Some frame dialogue around tolerance, others focus on overcoming fundamentalism, while others talk about focusing on compromise in the area of freedom of expression.[298] These models are built to address the power imbalance often present in dialogues between Muslims and the West, and seek to focus on social justice that does not exclude minority groups but builds on a vision of common humanity.[299] The promising development is that interfaith programs are recognising the need to have more integration of the Muslim perspective to enhance the effectiveness of dialogue. While there is work to be done, the increase in Muslim participation, and the advancements in Islamic models, all suggest that there is potential for a wider breadth of diplomatic policies in the future, impacting more regions and engaging more groups.

3.7 *Key Characteristics of Interfaith Dialogue*

When examining interfaith dialogue through its various methods and cultural perspectives, there are several consistent characteristics that are supported as imperative to effective dialogue. A key feature of interfaith dialogue is that it develops tolerance between groups as a way to avoid escalation of conflict and promote peaceful coexistence in society. Tolerance in the contemporary setting is described as "the mutual respect and cooperation between groups of different communities both in ethnicity, language, culture, politics,

295 Pallavicini, "Interfaith Education: An Islamic Perspective," 425.
296 Ibid., 428.
297 Ibid., 431.
298 Each of these models are explored fully in Zia-ul-Haq, "Muslims' Participation in Interfaith Dialogue: Challenges and Prospects," 640-641.
299 Ibid., 643.

and religion" and is "based on the principle of mutual respect."[300] The concept of tolerance is congruent with themes of religion and thus is evident in many teachings in religion.[301] However, the impact of interfaith dialogue can be felt beyond just achieving tolerance as its primary goal. In fact, as Mendes-Flohr identifies, "genuine interfaith dialogue acknowledges differences and celebrates our distinctive paths to the life of the spirit as refracting our shared humanity."[302] In fact, tolerance has often translated into indifference, where parties tolerate other groups at a distance without genuinely developing relations.[303] Tolerance is an important component of successful dialogue, but the impact can be much more far-reaching. Tolerance does still, however, need to be achieved within society. Typically, Western democracies struggle with building tolerance in society in times of peace, with antisemitism and Islamophobia being examples of how intolerance can permeate through societies and ultimately perpetuate cycles of conflict.[304] The pursuit of tolerance is an integral aspect of interfaith dialogue, but the outcomes of dialogue will be much more far-reaching if tolerance is one part of a broader strategy.

Another feature of interfaith dialogue that is accepted as a central goal is clarifying 'the other'. This works toward mediating estrangement and easing divisions between groups. At its core, this goal is about developing a genuine understanding between parties. To do this, participants must gather and disseminate information about the other religious tradition and potentially identify areas of theological convergence.[305] At a deeper level, the pursuit of understanding can be quite reflexive. This means that the participant will also evaluate their own personal beliefs and practices, which allows for the development of mutual relations between parties.[306] Ultimately, developing understanding between parties "involves a transformation of one's own beliefs while engaging with someone of another faith."[307] Burrell recognises that a by-product of interfaith dialogue is that dialogue can "be our beginning to see ourselves through the eyes of the other," which he notes is a pervasive

300 Christian, "Pluralism and Religious Tolerance in Indonesia: An Ethical-Theological Review Based on Christian Faith Perspectives," 349.

301 Ibid., 349.

302 Paul R. Mendes-Flohr, "Reflections on the Promise and Limitations of Interfaith Dialogue," *European Judaism* 46, no. 1 (2013): 4.

303 Mahmoud Ayoub, "9/11 and the Need for a New Paradigm for Interfaith Dialogue," *Muslim World* 101, no. 3 (2011): 562.

304 Sheetz-Willard et al., "Interreligious Dialogue Reconsidered: Learning from and Responding to Critique and Change," 266-268.

305 Neufeldt, "Interfaith Dialogue: Assessing Theories of Change," 349.

306 Ibid., 349.

307 Ibid.

issue in the West in terms of the misrepresentation of Muslim communities.[308] Most of the strategies and methods of interfaith dialogue are built in a way that the other is clarified and that is a successful outcome of interfaith dialogue which can be translated to other diplomatic contexts.

A chief goal that has been reinforced through the development of interfaith dialogue is the pursuit of pluralism within the community. This comes as a result of deeper dialogue and is fostered when groups move beyond exclusivism.[309] Scholars state that pluralism essentially levels the playing field across society and breaks down the barriers that have been built up and entrenched through divisions between religious groups.[310] When applied to dialogue, pluralism enables reconciliation, effective peacebuilding, and mutual charity between groups.[311] Patel applies a three-part framework for pluralism, being:

1. Respect for diverse identities;
2. Nurturing relationships between different communities;
3. Cultivating a commitment to the common good.[312]

Johanson examines pluralism from the Islamic perspective and highlights that the praxis for pluralism in Islamic tradition is more evident than some accept. However, it does still need to be made into a more concrete experience that builds on these scholarly findings.[313] To motivate communities toward accepting a pluralistic viewpoint, the understanding of pluralism is generally associated with five 'civic goods'. These are:

1. Increasing understanding and reducing prejudice. Prejudice works in opposition within a pluralistic society because it violates the rights of a target group and then raises barriers to their contribution which reinforces marginalisation.
2. Strengthening social cohesion and reducing the chances for identity-based conflict. By building diverse expressions of identity within the community, interfaith cooperation can be used as a vehicle to strengthen social cohesion and bridge discrepancies in social capital.
3. Building on the previous, bridging social capital and addressing social problems. Religiously pluralistic communities are able to work together

308 Burrell, "Christian-Muslim Dialogue in a World Gone Religiously Awry," 420.

309 Johanson, "Pluralistic Inclusivism and Christian-Muslim Dialogue: The Challenge of Moving Beyond Polite Discussion toward Reconciliation and Peace," 35.

310 Ibid., 35.

311 Ibid., 40.

312 Patel, "Preparing Interfaith Leaders: Knowledge Base and Skill Set for Interfaith Leaders," 77.

313 Johanson, "Pluralistic Inclusivism and Christian-Muslim Dialogue: The Challenge of Moving Beyond Polite Discussion toward Reconciliation and Peace," 45.

in a network to channel activities toward positive civic purposes, where interfaith leaders can target their progress to specific issues in the community such as poverty and disease.

4. Fostering the continuity of identity communities and reducing isolation. Interfaith leaders provide a framework, language and expression where those who identify with religious beliefs have a community to belong. It is important that people are not forced to stay within a community against their own will, but this notion of continuity aids in building cohesion in society and supporting plurality.
5. Creating binding narratives for diverse societies. Rituals, traditions and symbols can be found within religious identities that helps to reinforce notions of diversity within society. Done effectively, this diversity can help build a communal narrative which is in line with pluralistic thought.[314]

The pursuit of pluralism has become the goal of not just interfaith organisations, but it has become an integral feature of some states' policies. This is a prominent feature of Indonesian policy which will be examined later in this paper. However, constructing a method to establish pluralism is a significant aspect of the interfaith experience.

Another aim of developing interfaith dialogue is providing the conditions for genuine friendship to occur between groups. This is a by-product of dialogue of this nature, but the challenge has been understanding how to best fit friendship into the spectrum of practices and expectations, not only of conducting dialogue, but also of the nature of friendship itself.[315] Within religious traditions a basis for friendship can be found and if that is identified it can be fostered through dialogue. Friendship is achieved as part of a longer process which must be predicated on humility between parties as humility brings understanding and demonstrates the interconnected nature of some elements of religion, inducing empathy and leading to hospitality.[316] Hospitality is a theme that has garnered much academic attention with observers noting that scriptural teaching on giving hospitality is well-founded and could be a base to build cooperation between religious groups.[317] Another way that scholars recognise friendship can be developed is through gift giving and exchange

---

314 Patel, "Preparing Interfaith Leaders: Knowledge Base and Skill Set for Interfaith Leaders," 77-79.

315 "Interfaith Encounters between Jews and Christians in the Early Modern Period and Beyond: Toward a Framework," 378.

316 Burrell, "Some Requisites for Interfaith Dialogue," 310.

317 Omar, "Embracing the "Other" as an Extension of the Self: Muslim Reflections on the Epistle to the Hebrews 13:2," 439.

within dialogue.[318] There are several merits to friendship as a model for interfaith dialogue, as recognised by Dickens and Burrell who highlight that friendship provides a check against inclinations of self-deception and also strengthen the source of insights for the future.[319] Seeing interfaith dialogue as an exchange between friends moves past traditional foundationalist views,[320] which encourages dialogue to become and intersubjective encounter between persons.[321] Encouraging a platform to develop friendship through interfaith dialogue encourages long-term cooperation which can assist in abating communal issues.

An important consideration of interfaith dialogue is the level at which it is applied. Scholars recognise the importance of employing interfaith dialogue at the grassroots level, as this helps to build a fundamental peace and understanding among religious groups within the community.[322] Muwahidah reflects on the contributions of several authors who highlight the value of the grassroots approach of interfaith dialogue, including Küng's argument that interfaith dialogue can deal with concrete, philosophical, theological and textual problems at a communal level if fostered correctly.[323] Further, Swidler recognises that if interfaith dialogue is only left to scholars and religious leaders, the concerns of grassroots communities can be marginalised.[324] Muwahidah also echoed the sentiment of Kozlovic who recommended more research go into developing dialogical praxis at the grassroots level.[325] At the grassroots, however, there are a variety of different processes that can be employed. If the community chooses not to talk about particular religions, it should rather focus on broader themes within religion in general. However, the practitioner of interfaith dialogue must remember that the community defines its own values and norms, and these should not be imposed by someone outside of that community.[326] This is a growing trend that sees movements and organisations participate, namely from the local level. Dialogue is not promoted as a process for the elite

318 Ellen T. Charry, "Becoming Friends," *Journal of Ecumenical Studies* 50, no. 1 (2015): 118.

319 Dickens, "Frank Conversations: Promoting Peace among the Abrahamic Traditions through Interreligious Dialogue," 410.

320 Which Dickens describes as being "one either latches onto sure and certain knowledge that is universally available and incorrigible or slips into the abyss of sheer relativism where disagreements become arbitrary exercises of power". See ibid., 410.

321 Ibid., 410.

322 Muwahidah, "Interfaith Dialogue at the Grassroots Level: A Case Study of an Interfaith Empowerment Program in East Java, Indonesia," 79-80.

323 Ibid., 79-80.

324 Ibid., 79-80.

325 Ibid., 79-80.

326 Ibid., 91.

as the pressures from underrepresented groups has called for a seat at the table.[327] Grassroots approaches to conflict resolution and reconciliation are becoming more prominent in the literature, and grassroots forms of interfaith dialogue can also build on this trend.

Important to faith-based diplomacy is the involvement of religious leaders. They are also an integral asset to interfaith dialogue. Religious leaders are increasingly becoming a more important player in the construction of peace processes as they have the capacity to delegitimise actors who use violence to achieve their goals, but they can also provide nuanced advice to inform political negotiations, such as in truth and reconciliation commissions, or even by bringing different perspectives to the negotiating table.[328] While religious leaders have often released statements condemning terrorism, violence and conflict, there is the potential for those leaders to take active roles in addressing the religious factors of conflict.[329] They have often been the primary participant of interfaith dialogue and have successfully built networks of engagement and contributed to achieving the goals of dialogue. As they are prominent in interfaith dialogue, there is potential that their participation can translate into other forms of diplomatic strategy.

A key feature of interfaith dialogue which is growing in the literature is the place of dialogue in peacebuilding. When observing interfaith dialogue as a process of peacebuilding, there are four primary aims that can be achieved. Neufeldt states that these four aims are:

1. To alter attitudes and perceptions of the 'other.'
2. To access and build upon people's deep spiritual beliefs and motivations.
3. To broaden the participation of people building peace.
4. To develop a joint platform for actions to address the root causes of the conflict as well as its consequences.[330]

Each of these aims have been supported elsewhere in the literature on interfaith dialogue and demonstrate that interfaith dialogue can have an active role in the peace process if the dialogue is integrated effectively.

Abu-Nimer states that there are three categories of religious peacebuilding that generally occur. They include advocacy and human rights activities, dialogue and conflict resolution activities and, liberation and non-violent

327 Sheetz-Willard et al., "Interreligious Dialogue Reconsidered: Learning from and Responding to Critique and Change," 266.
328 Neufeldt, "Interfaith Dialogue: Assessing Theories of Change," 354.
329 For examples see Danforth, "Mobilizing Religion against Terrorism," 81.
330 Neufeldt, "Interfaith Dialogue: Assessing Theories of Change," 358.

resistance activities.[331] On the place of dialogue, he states that these activities "are carried out mostly through civil society groups and [nongovernmental organisations] to promote deeper understanding of the other, through skills training or dialogue encounters, and in some cases focus on specific issues of the conflict."[332] Focusing on peacebuilding within the conflict between Israel and Palestine, Kronish noted that interfaith institutions are able to move from dialogue to action, can address specific conflict issues, can focus on the larger community and not just an individual, and also develop long-term programs and relationship to ensure that the resolutions are enduring.[333] This shows that interfaith dialogue can be a part of a targeted peacebuilding strategy which may strengthen diplomatic outcomes.

Not only in peacebuilding is interfaith dialogue becoming a more prominent feature, but also in the broader conflict resolution context. Nationalism and ethnic conflict studies have been increasing, and the rise of identity dynamics in culture is becoming a more significant factor in conflict.[334] As a response to religious extremism in the Middle East following 9/11, research in the conflict resolution field has focused on terrorism and the potential that interfaith dialogue has in mitigating terrorism-related issues.[335] The scope of analysis in conflict resolution is expanding, and with identity and communal-based conflicts at the fore of analysis, the role of religion and interfaith dialogue will continue to be in the scope of analysis for some time. When applying this trend to faith-based approaches, faith-based peacebuilding is possible only when religious actors are committed to understanding and respecting the traditions of other religious groups. This common ground between religious traditions will allow for non-violent conflict transformation through forms of dialogue and reconciliation, which are already recognised as central processes of peacebuilding.[336] Religious leaders are also able to demonstrate their commitment to peacebuilding and reconciliation which traverses over religious boundaries to assist the community in moving toward genuine conflict resolution.[337] Increasingly, interfaith activities and declarations are

331 Mohammed Abu-Nimer, "Religious Leaders in the Israeli-Palestinian Conflict: From Violent Incitement to Nonviolence Resistance," ibid., no. 4. 561.

332 Ibid., 561.

333 Ron Kronish, "Interreligious Dialogue in the Service of Peace," *Cross Currents* 58, no. 2 (2008): 228.

334 Nimet Beriker, "The Conflict Resolution Field: Reflections on Multiple Realities, Challenges, and Geographical Divides," (Brown University, 2015), 17.

335 Ibid., 17.

336 Jari Portaankorva, "Muslim and Christian Leaders Working Together: Building Reconciliation in the Sierra Leone Conflict," *Journal of Pan African Studies* 8, no. 9 (2015): 80.

337 Ibid., 80.

highlighting peace as the main goal of dialogue. Institutions of political and religious natures have incorporated peacebuilding dimensions into interfaith dialogue. As the presence of religion in conflict is quite widespread, there is opportunity for these principles to continue to be integrated.[338] As the features of peacebuilding are becoming central goals of diplomatic strategy, incorporating interfaith dialogue as part of that strategy is increasingly more valuable.

While limited work has been done to incorporate interfaith dialogue as a diplomatic process, Mannion does propose combining the tracks of diplomacy with interfaith dialogue as a diplomatic tool. The tracks of diplomacy focus on different actors and how those actors might become involved in different forms of diplomacy and dialogue. The real challenge presented in the analysis of the tracks of diplomacy is bridging that gap between official state or institutional initiatives and grassroots initiatives, which is present when considering interfaith dialogue.[339] The analysis of the tracks of diplomacy highlight that the demarcation between official and unofficial diplomacy is no longer as rigid as it has been in the past, and that various groups can now work with official agents to participate in high-level discourse.[340] Interfaith dialogue can be the mode and vehicle for this intersection to be facilitated.[341] Essentially, Mannion expresses the value of the track 1.5 approach, that is the combining of official and unofficial diplomatic agents in the process of dialogue, maintaining that this approach should be utilised more in future.[342] By this example alone, it is evident that there is a natural convergence of diplomacy, faith-based approaches and interfaith dialogue that can be further strengthened.

3.8 *Actors and Agents of Interfaith Dialogue*

Clarifying the actors that engage in the interfaith approach, a recent trend is seeing international governmental organisations (IGOs) use their structures and mechanisms to promote and engage in interfaith dialogue. Of particular note is the interfaith dialogue sessions held by the United Nations in 2007 which aimed to create genuine dialogue between religions as a political instrument to "reach out across borders and build bridges of peace and hope."[343]

338 Sheetz-Willard et al., "Interreligious Dialogue Reconsidered: Learning from and Responding to Critique and Change," 266-268.

339 Mannion, "Pathways for Dialogue in the 21st Century: What We Learned at Assisi 2012," 394-395.

340 Ibid., 395-397.

341 Mannion defines the different tracks of diplomacy with certain references to interfaith dialogue bodies who have engaged with those various tracks, see ibid., 395-397.

342 Ibid., 399.

343 Neufeldt, "Interfaith Dialogue: Assessing Theories of Change," 344-345.

This work continued in 2008 where then Secretary-General Ban Ki-moon opened the United Nations High-Level Meeting on Interfaith Dialogue by stressing the need for groups to come together in respect and understanding, noting that "interfaith initiatives are addressing this need with ever greater frequency."[344] Along with IGOs, various other institutions have long been incorporating the processes of interfaith dialogue. An example of this often referred to in scholarship is the World Council of Churches and more recently their Office on Interreligious Relations and Dialogue. Neufeldt reflects on the Office's 'Thinking Together' series that brought together small groups of participants to present a variety of theological perspectives on the issues that were being faced at the time.[345] As the structures of institutions respond to the growing need for interfaith dialogue, the opportunities for genuine dialogue can continue to grow. These structural elements of interfaith dialogue have seen a rise in institutions that are formulated to facilitate interfaith dialogue, in many cases expressly toward peace and conflict resolution. Kronish examines the Interreligious Coordinating Council in Israel as an example of an institution that has been built around creating avenues for dialogue to address conflict issues in Israel and Palestine.[346]

Another area that has gained attention in faith-related activities in diplomacy is the area of development and aid delivery. Backues notes that civil society and faith-based organisations are able to develop positive interfaith relations by delivering humanitarian assistance programs, which could be used as a vehicle to develop interfaith dialogue programs.[347] To improve the humanitarian approach to dialogue, Fountain draws on the experience from the Aceh tsunami, noting that the motivations of humanitarian aid workers are important when deploying them into the community, but beyond that attention needs to be given to the history, identity, and theology of actors to see how best they will integrate into the community they are engaged with.[348] Various different actors that impact the diplomatic landscape are already moving toward interfaith dialogue as a valuable method, but the integration of faith-based and interfaith activities can be improved.

344 Magonet, "The Growth of Interfaith Dialogue," 41-2.

345 Neufeldt, "Interfaith Dialogue: Assessing Theories of Change," 351.

346 Kronish, "Interreligious Dialogue in the Service of Peace," 226.

347 Lindy Backues, "Interfaith Development Efforts as Means to Peace and Witness," *Transformation: An International Journal of Holistic Mission Studies* 26, no. 2 (2009).

348 Philip Fountain, "Mennonite Disaster Relief and the Interfaith Encounter in Aceh, Indonesia," *Asian Ethnology* 75, no. 1 (2016): 180.

3.9 *Strengths, Limitations and Recommendations for Interfaith Dialogue*

With the various components and actors of interfaith dialogue examined, the next sections will summarise on key strengths, limitations and recommendations for interfaith dialogue. Some of the strengths of interfaith dialogue include the fact that group cohesion within communities is developed, and this then aids in creating a unified group response to threats that may arise from conflict and division.[349] A strength from the growth of interfaith dialogue is that it has also prompted strategies of intra-faith dialogue, resolving tensions within different religious traditions. Argon notes that "the wider Muslim community presently consists of variegated communities and movements with uncoordinated and un-integrated smaller strategies" which can often be interpreted as divisiveness within the Muslim community, but the promotion of strategies in interfaith systems has presented channels of communication for these issues to be addressed.[350] Interfaith dialogue also has the capacity to respond to global events and develop a strong catalyst for reconciliation. Ariel recognised this following the Second World War, where Western Christian and Jewish communities had their relations restored and transformed due to the processes of interfaith dialogue.[351] The same response has been seen following 9/11 as interfaith dialogue can be seen as a vital tool in responding to global events. The processes of interfaith dialogue causes participants to confront questions of 'religious otherness' and examine the possibilities of religious diversity, where relationships between groups can assist in guiding through some confronting issues within society.[352] From a psychological perspective, Holland and Walker recognise that,

> If the need for relationship is not being met, then individuals can engage in either effective or non-effective behaviours to alleviate the pain. Through interfaith dialogue, participants are developing the skills to communicate with other people, including their need for relationship, in a way that is respectful and non-judgemental.[353]

349 Orton, "Interfaith Dialogue: Seven Key Questions for Theory, Policy and Practice," 350.

350 Argon, "Strategies for Interreligious and Inter-Muslim Dialogue: A Proposed Methodology," 365.

351 Ariel, "Interfaith Dialogue and the Golden Age of Christian-Jewish Relations," 1.

352 Holland and Walker, "Choice Theory and Interfaith Dialogue: Building Relationships between Faiths and Embracing Diversity," 19-20.

353 Ibid., 19-20.

This is a significant development in terms of the individual, but it also has implications that can flow on into community development and ultimately assist in alleviating tensions where the model works productively. These, along with key strengths identified throughout the analysis of interfaith dialogue, demonstrate the potential effectiveness of incorporating interfaith dialogue into diplomatic strategy. However, as with other potential strategies, there are inherent limitations that must be managed to ensure that the incorporating of interfaith dialogue does not have a harmful impact.

There are several limitations that must be accounted for when considering initiating dialogue. Due to the nature of interfaith dialogue, there will always be pressure placed on the motivations of beginning new interfaith initiatives, along with concerns about the legitimacy of key players participating in the interfaith process.[354] This relates to the idea of representation and who would be genuinely credible and legitimate as a representative of complex religious identity.[355] From this basis, another major limitation facing interfaith dialogue is the complexities inherent when developing an interfaith approach. The practitioner must consider the participants, the structure and the themes to be discussed within the dialogue.[356] Participants can range from local believers to high-level religious figures. The dialogue can take place on various levels, whether local or international, bilateral or multilateral. The themes can focus on ethical concerns, spiritual or theological issues, or even community challenges. When all of these factors are considered it becomes clear that the construction of interfaith dialogue is complex and multifaceted. Thus, when seeking to integrate interfaith dialogue into a diplomatic strategy, these various factors should be taken into account. From these factors, however, interfaith dialogue can still manifest in various different forms. Orton provides some examples, being that academics can exchange religious ideas, grassroots groups can target specific communal issues, consultation between religious leaders can inform diplomatic processes, and religious figures can share their experiences relating to religious practices.[357] While this broad spectrum of opportunities can be seen as a variety of positive avenues for observers to pursue, Orton notes that "the implications of this diversity remain highly contested in relation to policy and practice."[358]

354 Magonet, "The Growth of Interfaith Dialogue," 44.

355 Sheetz-Willard et al., "Interreligious Dialogue Reconsidered: Learning from and Responding to Critique and Change," 254-255.

356 Orton, "Interfaith Dialogue: Seven Key Questions for Theory, Policy and Practice," 351.

357 Ibid., 351.

358 Ibid., 351.

A poignant limitation in interfaith dialogue is that many observers perceive the process as a form of evangelisation or proselytization.[359] It is integral that dialogue is promoted in a way so as to not threaten participants with this as an outcome. The certainty of a participant's beliefs and values in a religious tradition should not be weakened through dialogue, but tolerance and open-mindedness can enable a more fruitful discussion.[360] Within the idea of proselytization is a persistent limitation in the development of interfaith dialogue has been that of conversion within interfaith settings. This does not only mean pursuing the conversion or proselytization of other participants but understanding the genuine nature of conversion within oneself. Religion and the conversion experience must be perceived as variegated and multifarious which allows participants to have respect and understanding for the positions of other interlocutors.[361] More specifically, if the dialogue is engaging with theological concepts and debate, there are some important points to consider. Historically there has been a reticence to engage in interfaith practices due to the participants feeling threatened of conversion. In studying this, Jacobs-Vendegeer impresses on participants who follow theological precepts, that missions and dialogue rest more in the hands of God than in the individual, and that this realisation results in humility which promotes engagement in dialogue for the purposes of engaging with other people.[362] It must be known among all parties that the purpose of interfaith dialogue is not to convert the other party to their own religious way of thinking, but rather to explore those differences and interests among all groups to foster mutual understanding. Adding to this difficulty is the potential for syncretism. This is an attempt to blend religious traditions to create a common sphere of beliefs. While interfaith dialogue aims to highlight areas of cooperation and support, syncretism dangerously blurs religious identities and is unequivocally rejected by religious leaders.[363] Balancing mutual exchange with this fear is a difficult task in interfaith dialogue but must be managed to achieve genuine dialogue.

After focusing primarily on the case of Arab-Jewish dialogue in the Middle East, Abu-Nimer identified several limitations that may be applicable in other

359 Sheetz-Willard et al., "Interreligious Dialogue Reconsidered: Learning from and Responding to Critique and Change," 254-255.

360 Mendes-Flohr, "Reflections on the Promise and Limitations of Interfaith Dialogue," 12.

361 Fridlund, "Double Religious Belonging and Some Commonly Held Ideas About Dialogue and Conversion," 274-5.

362 Christiaan Jacobs-Vandegeer, "Navigating the Circle of Interreligious Dialogue and Theologies of Religions," *Australian e-Journal of Theology* 19, no. 3 (2012): 216.

363 Mitwally Ibrahim, "Interfaith Dialogue a Muslim Legal Perspective on Its Validity, Concept and Practices," 125.

interfaith processes. First, he noted that interfaith groups are limited in their participants and that their focus of conversation is ritualistic and cultural explorations of other faith groups[364] This process does not actually address the structural violence in the Israeli-Palestinian context, which is why the dialogue must shift to focus on conflicting issues and theological similarities to begin bridging the gap between parties.[365] The interfaith groups have also gained a limited circle of followers, meaning that they rarely engage with new audiences which means the perspectives within the group stagnate.[366] Interfaith dialogue groups also have struggled to sustain and generate long-term impact as they are reliant on external funds and foreign agendas.[367] Internally, within the interfaith groups, there are challenges relating to reaching a wider audience while maintaining effectiveness with target groups, and also with financial transparency, and maintaining credibility within the community.[368] While these limitations have been drawn from one specific conflict example, there are several points that are helpful to be aware of when considering the effectiveness of interfaith dialogue in other conflict situations. Revealed from the Syrian cases of interfaith dialogue, a key limitation to successful dialogue is having unclear goals which infringe on participants being able to actively listen to each other.[369] This has led to fundamental miscommunications relating to social and political goals, ethical frameworks and accounts of history. It highlights the need for clear communication and articulation of the aims of interfaith dialogue, and the poignant reminder that parties need to be willing to listen to their interlocutors through dialogue.

The studies into these examples have produced a number of case-specific limitations. Generally, there is still significant mistrust between religious groups, namely when considering the perceptions of Muslims in the West, with empirical studies revealing low levels of optimism regarding dialogue between Muslim and the West, and even Muslim countries believing that interactions with Western states are in fact getting worse.[370] This has been supported by

364 Abu-Nimer, "Religious Leaders in the Israeli-Palestinian Conflict: From Violent Incitement to Nonviolence Resistance," 567-568.
365 Ibid., 567-568.
366 Ibid., 567-568.
367 Ibid., 567-568.
368 Ibid., 567-568.
369 Ali-Dib, "Inter-Religious Dialogue in Syria: Politics, Ethics and Miscommunication," 112.
370 Zia-ul-Haq, "Muslims' Participation in Interfaith Dialogue: Challenges and Prospects," 634-635.

the fact that interfaith dialogue has been Westernized, in that Western norms often underpin the processes and goals of the dialogue.[371]

Some still believe that the models and paradigms for interfaith dialogue focus too heavily on manufacturing tolerance but need to go beyond that to develop understanding and acceptance.[372] Critically, tolerance that has been developed in interfaith processes can be translated as indifference where the 'other' is merely tolerated to avoid conflict.[373] However, the interconnected nature of today's global society means this is no longer possible or desirable. This interconnectedness has resulted in a limitation that is becoming more pressing as a result of globalisation, what Fridlund calls 'double religious belonging.' Here, an individual may adhere to different religious traditions based on their own background or experiences and may apply different elements of those religious traditions based on personal needs.[374] Suomala also agrees with this difficulty in the complexity of religious identity, and notes that in this situation, the individual would likely not be invited to the table.[375] While this may promote an individual as interfaith within themselves, having that perspective in dialogue is complex, multifaceted, and may be difficult to incorporate within existing channels.

Through history, it has been apparent that oppressive forms of religion have pursued the interests of the religious elite at the expense of the individuals. While interfaith dialogue attempts to cross lines between religions, it is important that the dialogue take a liberating form, that is that it keeps in mind the needs and the participation of the individual and not just the religious elite.[376] This, Reiger discusses, is in line with the theology of the multitude, which encourages the multitude to engage in the practices of interfaith dialogue to assist in the affirmation of interfaith dialogue's central goals.[377] Elitism has been a common criticism of interfaith dialogue, with certain classes and titles being preferred over a broader participation base.[378]

371 Sheetz-Willard et al., "Interreligious Dialogue Reconsidered: Learning from and Responding to Critique and Change," 245-255.

372 Ayoub, "9/11 and the Need for a New Paradigm for Interfaith Dialogue."

373 Ibid., 562.

374 Fridlund, "Double Religious Belonging and Some Commonly Held Ideas About Dialogue and Conversion," 273.

375 Suomala, "Complex Religious Identity in the Context of Interfaith Dialogue," 360-361.

376 Joerg Rieger, "Occupy Religion: Theology of the Multitude and Interreligious Dialogue," *Buddhist-Christian Studies*, no. 34 (2014): 170.

377 Ibid., 171.

378 Sheetz-Willard et al., "Interreligious Dialogue Reconsidered: Learning from and Responding to Critique and Change," 254-255.

The most pressing limitation facing the advancement of interfaith dialogue is that many observers are pessimistic about the degree to which dialogue genuinely affects change in violent conflicts. Critics state that when interfaith dialogue fails it merely confirms the position that religious actors should not be involved in peacemaking, and when interfaith dialogue succeeds it is only viewed as 'a minor footnote.'[379] These limitations are presented to caution observers that interfaith dialogue is a complex program and, while it has the potential to support diplomatic strategy, must be constructed carefully to ensure that it achieves its intended goals. In light of these limitations, and the growing body of work on the topic, several authors have provided recommendations on how interfaith dialogue can be improved. This will strengthen the approach and ensure that it becomes a more workable strategy for diplomacy in the future. The following sections will propose a number of these recommendations.

In future, Orton recommends that those involved in the interfaith process avoid maintaining neutrality at the cost of bringing their own worldview and perspective into the dialogue in a healthy way.[380] This is an overcorrection to the point that groups in interfaith dialogue are only there to find common ground. To facilitate meaningful dialogue, it is imperative that those organising the dialogue recognise power relations and ethical issues that are inherent in practising within this field, including the policymaker's own identity, relationship building at a personal level, engage in reflexivity to assist in maintaining dialogue, and to be prepared for confronting questions relating to their own community.[381] On the other end of this spectrum, there must also be an awareness of narcissism, that is that scholars and practitioners would not get so focused on their own success that they fail to look beyond that and engage with other religions.[382] Indeed, participants must be willing to critique their own position, but remaining neutral for the sake of appeasing discussion weakens the outcome of dialogue.

A recommendation proposed by Neufeldt suggests that decisionmakers in the diplomatic and peacebuilding processes adjust their aim of interfaith dialogue. Research suggests that change must be achieved at the structural level.[383] This means that the aim of social cohesion is but a starting point as it does not effectively address the structural and systemic challenges of economic

379 Neufeldt, "Interfaith Dialogue: Assessing Theories of Change," 345.

380 Orton, "Interfaith Dialogue: Seven Key Questions for Theory, Policy and Practice," 362.

381 Ibid., 362.

382 Aihiokhai, "Going Beyond Nostra Aetate: The Way Forward for Interreligious Dialogue," 398.

383 Neufeldt, "Interfaith Dialogue: Assessing Theories of Change," 364.

disadvantage or political exclusion that often marginalises groups and leads to religious violence.[384] If interfaith dialogue can be recalibrated to address these targets specifically, the structural changes within the community may be sufficiently resolved before escalating into conflict.

Continuing in the peacebuilding perspective, Merdjanova proposes several recommendations to improve interfaith dialogue. First, observers must pay close attention to how interfaith dialogue is manipulated to ensure that it is firmly rooted in the analysis of political and economic conditions so that it can address structural issues. Furthermore, there should be a deeper incorporation of gender-critical dimensions to interfaith dialogue in peacebuilding. Another key recommendation is that the understanding and practice of interfaith dialogue could be expanded to consider 'interworldview dialogue' which integrates religious and secular participants. Finally, there should be a process of 'democratization' of dialogue so that participants can go beyond the binary and hierarchical representations of roles assigned within religious groups and broaden the base of participation from every level of society.[385]

In line with a growing trend in peacebuilding to seriously consider the role of women and integrate women into the multiple levels of decision-making. Interfaith dialogue can benefit from this same movement, by building connections between women's networks to strengthen existing channels and develop the understanding of what opportunities exist to create a sustainable peace with the inclusion of these different perspectives.[386]

Particularly within the area of responding to religious terrorism, religious communities have a variety of mechanisms by which they can spread anti-violence messages.[387] Groups should, however, be careful to develop a plan that is tailored to their own context, including the use of appropriate literature, media channels and mobilisation of workers.[388] While a unified, global message against terrorism would be ideal, it would require significant fundraising and expertise to be effective on the international stage.[389]

Practically, when applied to examples within a state, Borelli proposed a number of recommendations to improve interfaith dialogue between Christianity and Islam in the United States. One recommendation focused on looking at the relationship of religious groups to the contemporary world, being how do

384 Ibid., 364.

385 Merdjanova, "Overhauling Interreligious Dialogue for Peacebuilding," 30-32.

386 SumantO Al Qurtuby, "Religious Women for Peace and Reconciliation in Contemporary Indonesia," *International Journal on World Peace* 31, no. 1 (2014): 52.

387 Danforth, "Mobilizing Religion against Terrorism," 80.

388 Ibid., 80.

389 Ibid., 80.

religious groups fit in with consumerism, globalisation, secularised media, and so on.[390] Believers calling for reform exist within both religious traditions, but this discussion has the potential to engage both parties toward a common future, highlighting similar views on understanding the messages both religions promote and the role that believers should play in delivering that.[391] Borelli also notes that along with these processes, comparative theology should be given special attention between Christians and Muslims, developing respect for language, methods and dialogue between partners.[392] While this approach is possibly the most common through interfaith processes, it does serve a specific purpose in achieving the goals of interfaith dialogue, and should be evaluated to ensure that it is being conducted in best practice.

While interfaith dialogue found its base in theological debate and discussions within religious studies, there is an increasing need to move beyond just theological discussion as the goal of interfaith dialogue.[393] This is why Baum suggests that interfaith dialogue can be strengthened by incorporating thoughtful secular thinkers to bring social science methodology and non-theological factors into the dialogue process to achieve stronger outcomes.[394] This notion of extending an invitation to secular participants is something that was Pope Benedict pursued, where he invited secular contributions to speeches and conferences to broaden the perspectives offered and symbolically listen to the voices of those excluded.[395] Academic work is also developing on the nature of friendship within dialogue, and practical strategies, such as the exchanging of gifts, are being recognised as helpful in countering enmity between groups.[396] Whether the participants are from differing religious groups, or even taken from secular organisations, developing friendship between parties will help achieve the goals of dialogue. Even considering the advancements made in the processes of interfaith dialogue, more intensive mapping of dialogues is required, especially when considering the involvement of non-Biblical traditions, which is becoming more prominent in the current international environment.[397]

390 Borelli, "Christian-Muslim Relations in the United States: Reflections for the Future after Two Decades of Experience," 328.

391 Ibid., 328.

392 Ibid., 329-330.

393 Baum, "Interreligious Dialogue Includes Listening to Secular Voices," 363.

394 Ibid., 363.

395 Ibid., 367.

396 Charry, "Becoming Friends," 118.

397 Dakake, "A Good Word Is as a Good Tree: A Muslim Response to the Interfaith Challenges of Vatican II," 198.

The new media and social media landscape can be a great facilitating tool to proliferate messages in grassroots efforts, disseminating information and organising networks to assist in interfaith programs.[398] Groups are also focusing on activism to characterise their activities. This helps to narrow the focus of the organisation, concentrate on thematic issues which can help bypass the usual areas of stalemate in discussion, confront elitism by engaging in a broader participation which can cross tensions even from within one specific religious tradition.[399] These trends are unique to the trends in the contemporary international system and methods of interfaith dialogue will need to be constructed to meet these challenges.

More conceptually, Irmgedruth notes several different resources present within interfaith cultures which should be recognised in the future of interfaith exchanges. These include flexibility surrounding different individuals and their various perspectives, incorporating a large number of participants from the community to enact interfaith initiatives instead of forming exclusive dialogues, remember to quell intra-faith concerns before projecting them to the interfaith context, and support other dialogues that may not involve one's own religious perspective to help undermine the tendency to view groups as 'the other.'[400] Building on these developments, Miller proposes that interfaith reflection, "where researchers access resources from other faith traditions" is a more nuanced aspect of interfaith dialogue which has three distinct advantages. The first is that the goals of interfaith reflection are smaller and allow for definitive and achievable outcomes. The second is that this process doesn't struggle with differences but can look to a common goal and offer transformative possibilities between groups. The third is that this approach highlights a common humanity.[401] Miller puts this approach forward because the typical outcome of interfaith dialogue, as it is presently understood, is still limited by differences and entrenched disagreements. This notion of reflection, while being called upon by other scholars, can offer a perspective that goes beyond the traditional battlelines of disagreement.

3.10 *Cases of Interfaith Dialogue*

These recommendations have focused on specific areas in research that scholars have identified will assist in enhancing the theory and practice of interfaith

398 Sheetz-Willard et al., "Interreligious Dialogue Reconsidered: Learning from and Responding to Critique and Change," 266-268.

399 Ibid., 266-268.

400 Irmgedruth, "The Religious Challenge: To Live in the Context of Diverse Cultures," 59.

401 Miller, "Interfaith Dialogue in a Secular Field," 836.

dialogue. Other recommendations, for the improvement of interfaith dialogue, will come from examining cases where policies and programs have been initiated. These programs have sat within broader foreign policy and diplomacy strategies helpfully provide examples for how interfaith dialogue can be incorporated. This paper will focus on Indonesia and the United States as featured case studies, but there are other states worth mentioning that have made a notable contribution to the area of interfaith dialogue. While these cases will not be expounded on in great detail, they will be referenced here as they have demonstrated capacity and commitment to interfaith dialogue.

One of these states is Egypt. Mandour highlighted that Egypt has promoted an influential model of interfaith dialogue that brings intellectuals to the table, using scholarly contributions to promote the message of tolerance, justice and equity while building avenues for communication between interested parties that later become the basis for dialogue.[402] Upon this foundation communities have been able to discuss world religions, cultures and civilisations, developing a deeper understanding of core beliefs of different groups, which has seen Egypt become a more prominent player in the processes of interfaith dialogue.[403] Since the early 1990s, Egypt has worked to build channels of communication, host and participate in dialogue focused events and conferences, and export these processes to other parts of the world.[404] Egypt's position in the global system, particularly pertaining to interfaith exchange, makes them a valuable influencer among Arab states.

A prominent focal point of interfaith dialogue is the conflict in Israel-Palestine, witness to the clash of perspectives between three of the world's major religions. Interfaith activities have long been promoted in this region to alleviate tensions, but there are some complexities to this process. Abu-Nimer notes that the fundamental motivation for the different religious groups entering into dialogue is different. This has often resulted in ineffective initiatives. For the Palestinians, political change is the goal and thus they focus on structural causes to be addressed, while other Palestinians see interfaith dialogue as a way to be a participant in the process as their protests have gone unrecognised.[405] Jewish participants, however, focus on rehumanising

402 Mandour, "Islam and Religious Freedom: Role of Interfaith Dialogue in Promoting Global Peace," 890.
403 Ibid., 890.
404 Mandour's article explains, in great detail, a number of these events. See ibid.
405 Abu-Nimer, "Religious Leaders in the Israeli-Palestinian Conflict: From Violent Incitement to Nonviolence Resistance," 562-563.

and reducing prejudice, learning how to understand 'the other'.[406] These motivations must be clearly understood and the structures of dialogue need to be adjusted accordingly to ensure that their conversation avoids deadlock. While the scope for this paper, however, does not allow for the complexity of this case to be fully explored, the work on conflict resolution in Israel-Palestine is substantial, with interfaith dialogue playing a part in that process.

Other examples include the pursuit of friendship through dialogue in the conflict between Christianity and Islam in Nigeria.[407] The Netherlands has also worked actively to integrate faith groups into dialogue processes to address certain issues in their society, namely the cohesive integration of migrants in the community.[408] Portaankorva writes on the reconciliation process within Sierra Leone following their conflict and highlights the fact that religious groups were instrumental in supporting the work of the Truth and Reconciliation Commission within the community, as religious leaders worked hard to support dialogue efforts and encourage the community toward genuine restorative justice and post-conflict rebuilding.[409] The conflict in Syria has also garnered attention in the area of interfaith dialogue. The Syrian case of dialogue has, however, revealed discrepancies in what the parties are pursuing as their ultimate vision, resulting in divergent strategies which have been reinforced by different ethical traditions.[410] These examples demonstrate the capacity for interfaith programs to be tailored to focus on addressing specific issues pertinent within the context of a country.

An interesting example that draws out the Buddhist perspective of interfaith dialogue comes from Myanmar. Patterns of abuse, intolerance and discrimination have been inherent within Myanmar as a consequence of intense and violent conflict over time, and interfaith dialogue was suggested as a positive process to engage religious leaders with the political regimes at various levels to protect the rights and freedoms of the community and develop a sense of security within society.[411] From the Buddhist perspective,

---

406 Ibid., 562-563.

407 See SimonMary Asese Aihiokhai, "'Love One Another as I Have Loved You': The Place of Friendship in Interfaith Dialogue," (University of Pennsylvania Press, 2013).

408 See Freek L. Bakker, "Inter-Religious Dialogue and Migrants the Case of the Netherlands," *Mission Studies: Journal of the International Association for Mission Studies* 31, no. 2 (2014).

409 Portaankorva, "Muslim and Christian Leaders Working Together: Building Reconciliation in the Sierra Leone Conflict," 89.

410 Ali-Dib, "Inter-Religious Dialogue in Syria: Politics, Ethics and Miscommunication," 95.

411 Saw Hlaing Bwa, "Why Interfaith Dialogue Is Essential for Myanmar's Future," *Review of Faith & International Affairs* 13, no. 4 (2015): 75.

a harmonious society is pursued as a goal, and dialogue allows the discussion of shared values to penetrate the stagnated discussion of resolving conflict.[412] The primary target is building an inclusive and participatory society, where religious freedom has been set as a goal to build tolerance and enhance prospects of a robust democracy.[413] Contemporary developments in Myanmar's interfaith activities, in Hlaing Bwa's perspective, is the sign of a positive future where the people of Myanmar can engage more positively with their political authorities.[414]

The brief references to different examples here serve to demonstrate that the methods, goals, aims and central tenets of interfaith dialogue have already begun to translate into policies. Interestingly, while there is evident similarity between interfaith dialogue and programs of faith-based diplomacy, the link has not yet been firmly established. The remainder of this paper will explore the Indonesian and American experiences of integrated interfaith dialogue into policy to draw lessons on how to incorporate interfaith dialogue in the most effective way. Case studies have been the chosen methodology to understand the practice of interfaith dialogue. These case studies are descriptive in design as they seek to portray the broad array of programs and policies utilised by states in relation to interfaith dialogue. By examining journal articles, government programs and scholarly works on interfaith programs in these states, these cases will investigate in which ways, and how effectively, these states have been able to engage with interfaith dialogue as part of their diplomatic strategies. The case study methodology selected also reinforces the constitutive approach taken through this paper. As discussed in the introduction, constitutive theory provides understanding through description.[415] These case studies are not testing a causal hypothesis, but rather are describing the constitutive parts of interfaith dialogue in the countries being examined. Interfaith dialogue in Indonesia, for example, is not being assessed in terms of what caused it, or even in testing its effectiveness. Rather, this constitutive approach to case analysis is describing what interfaith dialogue is within the state, what elements make it up, and how it works within the case. As a result, observers will be able to see the variety of strategies and programs available for incorporating interfaith dialogue into diplomatic strategy, being the central goal of this paper.

412 Ibid., 76.
413 Ibid., 78.
414 Ibid., 78.
415 Wendt, "On Constitution and Causation in International Relations," 108.

4 Interfaith Dialogue: the Indonesian Experience

This section will examine the Indonesian experience of interfaith dialogue to highlight the practical implications of how these programs may assist in resolving conflict and enhancing societal cohesion. The Indonesian case is important due to their own national structures being built in a way that encourages quality interfaith dialogue. Religion has, since the early stages of nation-building in Indonesia, been politicised. Pedersen highlights that it is the world's most populous Muslim state, yet it is constitutionally secular, it has civil rather than Islamic law, it recognises six official world religions, and yet religion has been a driving factor to much of the conflict seen in the state.[416] In support, Sunarko finds that "in the Indonesian context, the adherents of different religions are challenged to dialogue and cooperate positively in the development of its unique form of democracy."[417] As such, Indonesia is unique when compared to other Muslim-majority countries in the international system as other religious groups have played a prominent role in the affairs of the nation, buttressed by Indonesia's Pancasila political ideology which is underpinned by religious freedom and equality among citizens.[418] Suharto's regime collapse in 1998 brought about movements of religiously fuelled violence, which have tested Indonesia's pluralist reputation.[419] Essentially, the transition to democracy "has been accompanied by a 'conservative turn' in Islam, and a new swing towards religious intolerance, marked by the state's failure to protect minorities and to bring perpetrators of discrimination and violence to justice."[420]

In general, Indonesia is positioned to use interfaith dialogue as a way to develop tolerance and harmony between believers as experiences in the past in Indonesia have focused on collaboration to solve issues of "social injustice, terrorism, secularism, materialism, hedonism and consumerism that threaten the life of humankind."[421] This type of issues-based dialogue has been successful in the Indonesian context and has been underpinned by a myriad of norms

---

416 Lene Pedersen, "Religious Pluralism in Indonesia," *The Asia Pacific Journal of Anthropology* 17, no. 5 (2016): 387.

417 Sunarko Ofm, "Interfaith Dialogue and Cooperation across Faiths: The Experience of Indonesia," 46.

418 Robert W. Hefner, "Christians, Conflict, and Citizenship in Muslim-Majority Indonesia," *Review of Faith & International Affairs* 15, no. 1 (2017): 91.

419 Ibid., 91.

420 Parker, "Religious Education for Peaceful Coexistence in Indonesia?," 487.

421 Christian, "Pluralism and Religious Tolerance in Indonesia: An Ethical-Theological Review Based on Christian Faith Perspectives," 355.

to garner the support of society and official agents. This does not, however, mean that there have not been challenges in Indonesia's policies on interfaith dialogue.

Indonesia had to overcome violent conflict to fully realise the potentialities of interfaith dialogue. When President Suharto resigned from power in 1998, sectarian, ethno-religious and communal conflict escalated across the nation. Of note was the violence in Ambon and Maluku where thousands died and at least one-third of the population was displaced.[422] This was, in the opinion of some scholars, the first large-scale case of Christian-Muslim violence in Indonesia, at least since the military activity in East Timor and the anti-Communist violence in 1965.[423] Despite Indonesia's reputation as a generous and tolerant nation, there are significant regional trends in Indonesia as over 80 per cent of incidents involving religious intolerance have occurred in Aceh, West Java and South Sulawesi.[424]

A recent example of religious freedom in Indonesia that has garnered international attention involves the case of blasphemy during the 2017 election of the Governor of Jakarta. Families of former presidents, protests across the countries and formal investigations of religious leaders saw Governor Ahok jailed, polarising opinions within Indonesia.[425] This was a result of comments made by Ahok on Quranic verses during the campaign in 2016. The ensuing tension surrounding this case saw divides between legal perspectives, political structures and society in general and demonstrates the need for religious freedom and interfaith programs to be a consistent feature in Indonesian society. This case notwithstanding, Indonesia's structures and institutions are open to seeing interfaith dialogue as a central feature of Indonesian society. Take, for example, the Institute for Interfaith Dialogue in Indonesia, which began in 1991 and has since conducted a variety of different programs to promote the values of religious pluralism and demonstrate that interfaith dialogue is necessary.[426] The culture of interfaith dialogue in Indonesia has been developed over time, buttressed significantly by government policies.

More formally, these policies that support interfaith dialogue are embedded in the official philosophical foundation of the Indonesian state, Pancasila.

---

422 Al Qurtuby, "Peacebuilding in Indonesia: Christian–Muslim Alliances in Ambon Island," 351.

423 Ibid., 351.

424 See Paul Marshall, "The Ambiguities of Religious Freedom in Indonesia," *The Review of Faith & International Affairs* 16, no. 1 (2018): 91.

425 Ibid., 92.

426 Achmad Munjid, "Building a Shared Home for Everyone – Interreligious Dialogue at the Grass Roots in Indonesia," *Journal of Ecumenical Studies* 43, no. 2 (2008): 1.

Pancasila translates as 'Five Principles' and comprises of five principles that underline the Indonesian state, being: (1) belief in the one and only God; (2) just and civilized humanity; (3) the unity of Indonesia; (4) democracy guided by the inner wisdom in the unanimity arising out of deliberations amongst representatives; and (5) social justice for all of the people of Indonesia.[427] This approach, as the foundation to Indonesian society, is "a valuable tradition" which anticipates the "important ethnic and religious problems" Indonesia faces as a pluralistic nation.[428] It aims to accommodate diversity within Indonesia and offer a framework for different groups to coexist.[429]

The first principle of Pancasila obviously has garnered some debate in terms of allowing for adherents from other religions being fully integrated into Indonesian society and culture, with Islamic groups often seeking to protect this position.[430] Yet, the overriding pursuit of a just and plural culture recognises that Indonesian society is unified under a God of their own religion. In essence, the first principle prohibits atheism with the Ministry of Religious Affairs extending official status to Islam, Catholicism, Protestantism, Buddhism and Hinduism. Other religions are able to register as social organisations with the Ministry of Culture and Tourism, which demonstrates that there is still some separation between religious groups, but that the Pancasila doctrine is fundamentally pluralistic.[431] The Ministry of Religious Affairs in Indonesia has existed since 1945 and has worked with two primary goals being to organise the hajj and govern religious education, along with providing the necessary processes to authorise religious identity and fund communities to build places of worship.[432] In comparison to other countries in the world, Indonesia has done well to manage the pluralistic nature of a mule-religious society and has used political philosophy to underpin those advancements. As a result of Pancasila, many interfaith programs have been able to gain favour within the Indonesian state.

As a central goal of interfaith dialogue, and as a priority within Indonesian community, pluralism is a key aspect of Indonesia's interfaith experience. The challenges of religious plurality are evident in South Asia and Southeast Asia

427 Sunarko Ofm, "Interfaith Dialogue and Cooperation across Faiths: The Experience of Indonesia," 53.

428 Ibid., 58-59.

429 Parker, "Religious Education for Peaceful Coexistence in Indonesia?," 488-489.

430 Sunarko Ofm, "Interfaith Dialogue and Cooperation across Faiths: The Experience of Indonesia," 53.

431 Muwahidah, "Interfaith Dialogue at the Grassroots Level: A Case Study of an Interfaith Empowerment Program in East Java, Indonesia."

432 Parker, "Religious Education for Peaceful Coexistence in Indonesia?," 488-489.

as religious groups are in a time of significant conflict.[433] Even in the face of these regional trends, Indonesia can provide a benchmark for structures and policies that can support religious plurality within a state and move away from religious violence. Historically, Indonesia has been able to promote a level of plurality as many of the state's indigenous cultures place great value on social harmony.[434] These local-level, historical trends of plurality do not preclude these religious groups for experiencing tension, namely regarding places of worship. However, there has been interesting trends in plurality between different groups for some time.[435]

In the reformation of Indonesian statehood, plurality became a central feature of Indonesian society. In fact, Soekarno asserted that the Indonesian nation believed in God and that Indonesians have a right to believing the God of their own religion, calling for Indonesia to be a nation where each worships as they choose, but Indonesia remains united as a religious country.[436] These clear statements of pluralism from the head of state permeate through the structures and cultures of Indonesian society. Inherent in Pancasila, namely the second principle, the founding architects of Indonesia's state philosophy recognised the socio-cultural and socio-economic diversity of Indonesia, and thus a sense of common humanity was necessary to preserve group harmony.[437] This led to a system of deliberative democracy that protected the pluralism inherent in Indonesian society.

There have been some challenges to Indonesian plurality. While the tradition of tolerance and plurality is longstanding in Indonesia, an Islamic resurgence since the 1980s has seen some Muslim groups within Indonesia discontented with their place in the Indonesian nation when compared to Muslim majority countries elsewhere.[438] Indonesia has also had the presence of militant fringe groups among Muslim populations, such as Darul Islam in the independence period of Indonesia to Jemaah Islamiyah in the early 21st century.[439] While these challenges have been present, the modern dynamics of religious plurality have allowed the positive elements of this Indonesian tradition to be maintained, also supported by Indonesia's commitment to attaining democracy.

433 See Javier, "Interreligious Dialogue: Historical Constants and Challenges in Asia," 240-244.

434 Marshall, "The Ambiguities of Religious Freedom in Indonesia," 85.

435 Pedersen, "Religious Pluralism in Indonesia," 393.

436 Sunarko Ofm, "Interfaith Dialogue and Cooperation across Faiths: The Experience of Indonesia," 53.

437 Ibid., 55.

438 Hefner, "Christians, Conflict, and Citizenship in Muslim-Majority Indonesia," 91.

439 Ibid., 91.

Following dramatic regime changes in Indonesia, democracy became a central feature of Indonesian statehood, and interfaith organisations have been avid contributors to promoting and protecting democracy.[440] One area to strengthen democracy has been ensuring the protection of religious freedoms. The notion of religious freedom enables plurality to exist without fear that it may be violated. With respect to religious freedom, the aftermath of Suharto's fall saw a strong promotion to encourage religious freedom and openness in Indonesian society. The national government under Susilo Bambang Yudhoyono, however, refused to intervene if the religious freedoms of communities were limited by local leaders and addressed the Indonesian Ulama Council's National Congress to give greater authority in defining what constitutes 'proper Islam.' In fact, the Council went so far as to issue a statement declaring that religious pluralism is prohibited in Islam.[441] Further, the government issued a regulation on houses of worship in 2006 which has limited how religious minorities have been able to express their faith. While President Widodo has been more positive in terms of protecting religious freedom, the situation at the grassroots remains quite tense.[442] While Indonesia has been able to withstand many challenges of conflict, analysts have stated that "the biggest issue for Indonesian democracy is not terrorism but intolerance, which is moving from the radical fringe into the mainstream" further substantiating the need for the country to maintain strong interfaith policies to safeguard its democracy into the future.[443]

Indonesia is the world's largest Muslim-majority state and resultantly, they do provide uniquely Islamic perspectives on interfaith dialogue. This means that there has been a strong exchange between religious traditions in Indonesia. For example, the Catholic Church was able to respond to the calls of the Vatican II Council and engage in interfaith dialogue, using their theology as a basis for community involvement.[444] Catholic and Protestant groups have placed a priority on affirming international human rights which also promoting indigenous precedents for multi-religious citizenship while also standing against anti-pluralist militias in certain parts of the country.[445]

---

440 Sunarko Ofm, "Interfaith Dialogue and Cooperation across Faiths: The Experience of Indonesia," 51.

441 Munjid, "Building a Shared Home for Everyone – Interreligious Dialogue at the Grass Roots in Indonesia," 1.

442 Marshall, "The Ambiguities of Religious Freedom in Indonesia," 86.

443 Hefner, "Christians, Conflict, and Citizenship in Muslim-Majority Indonesia," 97.

444 Sunarko Ofm, "Interfaith Dialogue and Cooperation across Faiths: The Experience of Indonesia," 46-50.

445 Hefner, "Christians, Conflict, and Citizenship in Muslim-Majority Indonesia," 98.

From a broader Christian perspective, there have been a number of responses offered by Christian organisations in relation to issues within Indonesia, namely challenges to citizenship. Hefner identifies some consistent trends in these responses. First, Christian groups have experienced periodic persecution, but they have not experienced historically systematic patterns of persecutions. Second, Christian and pluralist Muslim activists have recognised an increase in anti-Christian discrimination and violence since the democratic transition in 1998-1999. Third, these Christian activists note, however, that recent violence against smaller, isolated minorities, such as Shia minorities, has been far more severe than that experienced by the Christian population. Fourth, Christian leaders in Indonesia unequivocally maintain their goal of a multi-religious and pluralist Indonesia. They note that international campaigns and legal positions are important, however, the primary goal to secure this future is to cooperate with the majority of Indonesian Muslims that support the citizenship principles embedded in Pancasila.[446]

There is also a presence of misunderstanding between Jewish and Islamic communities within Indonesia, with academics and religious leaders working with religious passages to promote pluralism within society between these groups.[447] The shared principles of tolerance are yet to be fully disseminated into the communities within Indonesia, but dialogue has occurred between these religious communities to build a harmonious social life.[448] The awareness of the need to enhance interreligious cooperation is based on several factors. In Indonesia, there is support from the government that dialogue and understanding between religions should be pursued, along with a number of nongovernmental organisations that advocate for diversity and awareness with progressive interactions between groups moving all the way through the nation.[449] These factors make Indonesia a conducive environment for interfaith models to be developed, something that other nations can work from.

Beyond general characteristics of interfaith dialogue that are present in Indonesian society, there are a number of specific cases where interfaith dialogue was used as a part of conflict resolution strategies. For example, observers look to the Banyu Urip conflict of 1967 as a case of religious violence where dialogue has played a key role in conflict resolution processes. Essentially, a Christian missionary moved into the region and recruited villagers for

446 Ibid., 98.

447 Muhamad Ali, "'They Are Not All Alike'," *Indonesia & the Malay World* 38, no. 112 (2010): 339.

448 Ibid., 340.

449 Ibid., 345.

conversion, leaving New Order government officials in Java with violent attitudes toward this activity which resulted in massacres and violence between anti-communist, anti-atheist and religious groups alike.[450] This conflict event required a response that addressed the interfaith tension existing at its core. With specific reference to the methods of interfaith dialogue mentioned earlier, Muwahidah highlights 'liberative dialogue' as the model which brought together members of the community to move away from violence, firstly focusing on non-religious issues to promote communal harmony and then developing the relationship from that point.[451] This example demonstrates that the interfaith experience in Indonesia began early in the development of this area of analysis which might go to suggest why it has become embedded into Indonesian political thought.

Exploring the practical involvement from the Catholic perspective, Sunarko identifies six different examples of interfaith dialogue that were instigated in the Indonesian community following the Vatican II proposals. These are:

1. In 1966, the Supreme Council of the Indonesian Bishops (called MAWI) established a commission and a forum which aimed to promote interreligious dialogue systematically.
2. Further in 1966 MAWI asked for provincials of congregations to appoint or train experts on Islamic religion.
3. In 1970, 'Working Guidelines for Indonesian Catholics' were issued by MAWI to give a practical framework for interfaith cooperation in the community.
4. In 1985, a handbook on the relationship of church and state for Indonesian Catholics was published to encourage harmony between religious groups and government agents.
5. The Indonesian Bishops Conference (called KWI) advocated against state policies that seemed to target Indonesian pluralism. They compiled the complaints and delivered an annual report on religious freedom to the United Nations and used this as a way to protect religious human rights within Indonesian society.
6. KWI also cooperated with other religious institutions including Islamic organisations, Protestant groups and other nongovernmental organisations to build cohesion between interfaith groups in protecting religious rights and managing communal concerns.[452]

---

450 Muwahidah, "Interfaith Dialogue at the Grassroots Level: A Case Study of an Interfaith Empowerment Program in East Java, Indonesia," 83.

451 Ibid., 86.

452 Sunarko Ofm, "Interfaith Dialogue and Cooperation across Faiths: The Experience of Indonesia," 50-51.

Having a variety of long-standing interfaith programs in operation between the Catholic Church in a Muslim community shows the ways in which interfaith programs can be utilised to target shared issues within society.

The most prominent case of religious violence was In Maluku, where major religious and ethnic groups broke out in violence in 1999 and this was sustained for four years.[453] Three central factors were posited by Bertrand and supported by Al Qurtuby, as the cause of this conflict being: "(1) uncertainty over a secular definition of the nation that leaves open the query of an Islamic state, (2) patrimonial features of the authoritarian regime, and (3) a rapid democratic transition since the downfall of Suharto in May, 1998."[454] The escalation to conflict was also exacerbated due to uneven economic development, and elite agents of the central government driving the conflict, which aggravated the local communities.[455] The conflict in Maluku was concentrated in the city of Ambon, where 5,000 people died and 700,000 were displaced, where violence between Christian and Muslim groups was exacerbated due to discrepancies on a local level relating to socioeconomic status and political influence between the two groups.[456] The conflict was made more complex as it was not just a simple Christian-Muslim division between conflict parties. Ideological disputes between Muslim combatants, coming from different regions, brought division to the group which saw a separatist movement, Mujahidin groups, and foreign fighters from Mindanao and Afghanistan enter the fray.[457] This complicated the possibility for resolution as interreligious violence was sustained on multiple fronts. Factions on every side used religious ideas, texts and discourses to create a foundation to legitimise their cause which influenced the local groups.[458] Institutions struggled to manage the spread of violence and property, places of worship and other forms of infrastructure were destroyed, which further exacerbated post-conflict rebuilding efforts.[459]

From this experience of violent religious conflict, interfaith programs were developed to address the conflict issues. The example of successful interfaith

453 Al Qurtuby, "Peacebuilding in Indonesia: Christian–Muslim Alliances in Ambon Island," 351.

454 "Religious Women for Peace and Reconciliation in Contemporary Indonesia," 31.

455 Ibid., 32.

456 Agnieszka Kanas, Peer Scheepers, and Carl Sterkens, "Religious Identification and Interreligious Contact in Indonesia and the Philippines: Testing the Mediating Roles of Perceived Group Threat and Social Dominance Orientation and the Moderating Role of Context," *European Journal of Social Psychology* 46, no. 6 (2016): 700-702.

457 Al Qurtuby, "Peacebuilding in Indonesia: Christian–Muslim Alliances in Ambon Island," 352.

458 Ibid., 353.

459 "Religious Women for Peace and Reconciliation in Contemporary Indonesia," 30.

diplomacy between Muslim groups, Christian groups, religious actors, moderate factions of the government and civil society organisations was the signing of the Malino I and Malino II Peace Accords in 2001 and 2002 respectively.[460] These accords came as a response to violence that had occurred in Maluku and Sulawesi. While some religious actors were responsible for escalating conflict, other religious leaders were instrumental in contributing to conflict transformation and peacemaking efforts when violence broke out in 1999 with initiatives fostering local reconciliation.[461] In some parts of the region, religious actors were working independently from any support from government or nongovernmental organisations, and pursued interfaith dialogue of their own volition.[462] Malino II set out several primary goals including to end violence, support economic development, investigate where the conflict originated from, called for disarmament of rebel groups and minimise tensions.[463] A group that was instrumental in supporting the peace accords was the Peace Team of Wayame. These actors identify themselves as religious peacebuilders and sought to bridge social capital to create identities that could be modelled. They focused on building trust and friendship between groups to enhance the possibility of dialogue and reduce large-scale violence.[464] As a group derived from their local community, this peacebuilding body had grassroots impact and was recognised by government officials as key initiators of the peace process.[465]

In 2003, 40 Muslim and Christian leaders met in Central Maluku to engage in a five-day dialogue that focused on how to rebuild their community after conflict. The dialogue resulted in a shared narrative for reconciliation which, in the dialogue, was realised through four processes. First, groups were able to explore differences and common ground in their religious traditions. Second, groups identified shared religious values. Third, a common way of exploring significant differences between religious groups was developed. And fourth, urgency in transcending the conflict situation and rebuilding the community was promoted by all parties.[466] Practically, these motivations that underpinned the dialogue resulted in seven practical goals to achieve peace in the

460 "Peacebuilding in Indonesia: Christian–Muslim Alliances in Ambon Island," 349-350.
461 Ibid., 350.
462 Ibid., 350.
463 Ibid., 363.
464 Ibid., 362.
465 Ibid., 363.
466 Carmen Lowry and Stephen Littlejohn, "Dialogue and the Discourse of Peacebuilding in Maluku, Indonesia," *Conflict Resolution Quarterly* 23, no. 4 (2006): 409-410.

Maluku region. These goals reveal what interfaith dialogue can translate into when supported as a peacebuilding effort. These goals include:

1. Providing a space for community leaders to explore the conflict and pay attention to the religious components that influenced the conflict systems.
2. Provide participants from conflict-affected communities to co-create strategies that promote peace drawing on faith traditions, among other sources.
3. Build capacity of participation to engage in new dialogues between groups.
4. Identify specific activities to implement within a community to aid in recovery.
5. Promote interfaith coalition building between groups as a model to encourage reintegration and recovery.
6. Document processes and assess the impact of these processes in achieving the goals of strategies.
7. Disseminate those results to help others interested in peacebuilding dialogue.[467]

The dialogue was supported by a number of partnering nongovernmental organisations and agencies and successfully established collective goals, transformed the relationships of previously conflicting parties, and created the framework for future interactions.[468] This example demonstrates how interfaith dialogue can work within a broader diplomatic strategy as a peacebuilding strategy.

Another example of interfaith dialogue manifesting in Indonesia was evident when groups were responding to the Acehnese natural disaster in 2004. Various religious groups, in this case Christian groups, were using disaster relief as a mode of engaging in dialogue to build interfaith cohesion with the local Acehnese Muslims.[469] Where there might have typically been hostility, the priority of the faith-based organisations was to deliver aid, and thus the threat of proselytization was removed, softening locals into engaging with these groups in an interfaith exchange. This provided the platform for relationships to be developed and built upon post-disaster. A more niche example, perhaps, has been the joint program between an Indonesian Muslim music group and a Christian music group collaborating to express their identity through music,

467 Ibid., 412.

468 Ibid., 415.

469 Fountain, "Mennonite Disaster Relief and the Interfaith Encounter in Aceh, Indonesia," 179.

building religious identities and addressing harmful stereotypes.[470] This program took place in Yogyakarta, Java, and provides an example of Indonesia's willingness to invest into different interfaith methods to support dialogue and strengthen Indonesia's commitment to plurality.

While civil society organisations in many parts of the world have been integral to society, secular organisations have remained relatively weak in the Indonesian context, while citizens have actively supported the presence of faith-based organisations.[471] During the oppressive Suharto regime, civic activities were closely monitored, with the exception of religious activities. During the anti-Communist movement, the place of religion in society was made more important with policies, namely Pancasila, highlighting the key role that citizens and civil organisations play in achieving the goals of social harmony.[472] Interestingly, while Western societies see their faith-based organisations rely heavily on government funding, Indonesian communities actively support and resource their organisations, which means that they can operate with a level of separation from the government to achieve their programs.[473] This is a significant opportunity when considering the opportunities for interfaith dialogue in Indonesia. In the case of Islamic faith-based organisations, funded through zakat, Sakai highlights five key factors for their success in Indonesia. First, the Muslim-dominant society allows Muslim interests to be promoted through forms of popular media. Second, the middle-class Muslim communities have grown leading to new interpretations of Islamic theology. Third, professional networks and associations have been established which institutionalise the sector. Fourth, sources of funding have been widened to have several corporate donations flowing through as social responsibility legislation funnels into the community. Finally, Islamic theology suggests that the state should have management of zakat funds, but due to Indonesia not technically being an Islamic state, they have had to adjust their structures to allow privately run zakat collection agencies the legitimate status to run programs.[474]

While these examples highlight the success of interfaith dialogue in Indonesia to address social issues and assist in peace processes during and after conflict, there have been several challenges to interfaith dialogue in Indonesia. One such challenge facing Indonesian interfaith dialogue is cooperation that

470 King, "Music, Peacebuilding, and Interfaith Dialogue: Transformative Bridges in Muslim–Christian Relations," 313-314.

471 Minako Sakai, "Building a Partnership for Social Service Delivery in Indonesia: State and Faith-Based Organisations," *Australian Journal of Social Issues* 47, no. 3 (2012): 376.

472 Ibid., 376.

473 Ibid., 377.

474 Ibid., 379.

leads to the development of deep structures of democracy. In this, adherents from other religions must cooperate to with one another to enable and support the growth of new and stronger democratic structures within the state.[475] Indonesia has long been celebrated in terms of its democratic transition and even in the global shifting of the 'Arab Spring' movements in the world, Indonesia has maintained its commitment to democracy. The democratic transition, however, is challenged by deeper transitions to religiously equitable citizenship. Still, pro-pluralist organisations are working to see the pluralistic traditions in Indonesia realised in this time.[476] Another important factor to remember is that violent conflict of the nature experienced in Indonesia required a long time to heal, and in many cases reconciliation and trust-building process are still required in Indonesia to heal the trauma.[477] Even in light of these challenges, Indonesia has remained committed to upholding their policies of interfaith dialogue.

From these experiences, there are ways that Indonesia can improve their interfaith programs. From analysing the case of conflict in Indonesia, namely the Maluku case, Lowry proposes eight recommendations for the future of interfaith dialogue in Indonesia, but also in interfaith dialogue more broadly. Firstly, dialogue should be focused, targeted and well supported. Institutions should provide resources to support the goals of interfaith activities. Secondly, a diverse set of leaders should be integrated into the dialogue process. The complexity of conflict can be simplified by incorporating diverse perspectives. Thirdly, a safe environment should be provided, along with strong facilitation in the dialogue. Fourth, demonstrate to participants that their views are being heard and taken seriously. Listen, understand and acknowledge the participants as they engage in the dialogue process. Fifth, allow participants to assume ownership of the dialogue so that the goals of the dialogue reflect the hopes and aspirations of these community leaders. Facilitators should constantly allow for participants to express their desires and reflect on what has been discussed. Sixth, the dialogue should be framed around questions that will enable participants to go beyond the hostilities and disagreements between the groups. Seventh, incorporate local culture and religious traditions into the dialogue respectively. This means that differing perspectives and opinions are not ignored but celebrated as diversity brings a richness among

475 Sunarko Ofm, "Interfaith Dialogue and Cooperation across Faiths: The Experience of Indonesia," 58-59.

476 Hefner, "Christians, Conflict, and Citizenship in Muslim-Majority Indonesia," 100.

477 Al Qurtuby, "Religious Women for Peace and Reconciliation in Contemporary Indonesia," 33.

the participants and to the outcomes of the dialogue. Finally, dialogue sessions should be integrated into larger, ongoing peacebuilding efforts that have mechanisms to follow-up and track progress.[478]

The foundation for interfaith dialogue in Indonesia is well-established, however genuine interfaith dialogue will continue to play a pivotal role in Indonesia if it focuses on orienting toward public interests.[479] Essentially, Indonesia is in a unique position to have interfaith dialogue as a valid tool for not just discussions between religious groups, but as integral agents of change within society. A consistent recommendation in the area of interfaith dialogue is to enhance the role of women in conflict resolution and reconciliation. The Indonesian case is no different. While there is a gap in literature about the key role woman have played in reconciliation processes, there is distinct evidence that religious women were key peacebuilding agents in Ambon and other Moluccan islands, with members who fled the Maluku violence being supported by women in particular.[480] The women in this region are effective and entrepreneurial, thus able to address the underlying conflict issues, in their peacebuilding efforts and show similar traits as in other regions in Indonesia, with the potential for a strong network of peacemaking possible.[481]

As religious education has been a prominent feature of the structures the Indonesian state, Parker recommends that the area of religious education can be improved to have a participatory tolerance and critical interfaith component.[482] It should become practical and useful for educating young people on social diversity – reinforcing the principles of good citizenship underpinned by Pancasila.[483] While governments have been relatively inconsistent in how they seek to manage religious diversity, religious education within schools can must provide an interfaith component as opposed to mono-religious education programs to provide consistency in promoting religious plurality that can withstand the shifting of political administrations.[484] This does not just relate to schools, but also can be translated to higher education institutions in Indonesia, where state-run Islamic schools have long been prominent.

478 Lowry and Littlejohn, "Dialogue and the Discourse of Peacebuilding in Maluku, Indonesia," 423-425.

479 Sunarko Ofm, "Interfaith Dialogue and Cooperation across Faiths: The Experience of Indonesia," 58-59.

480 Al Qurtuby, "Religious Women for Peace and Reconciliation in Contemporary Indonesia," 29.

481 Ibid., 51-52.

482 Parker, "Religious Education for Peaceful Coexistence in Indonesia?," 494.

483 Ibid., 494.

484 Ibid., 495.

The disciplines taught, namely in areas of religious education, can incorporate interfaith considerations. Since the Reformation Era in Indonesia, Islamic colleges and universities have been able to engage in public discourse on the notions of multireligious citizenship from an Islamic perspective.[485] While these institutions have often recognised interfaith cooperation as a pillar of social harmony, the systems of Islamic higher education have been complicated by a broader social debate over what Islam looks like in the future of Indonesia. Nonetheless, these education institutions present an opportunity for engagement in a different light.

While interfaith policies have been an integral feature of Indonesia's domestic policies, there are opportunities for it to translate internationally. The most obvious case of this being successful in Indonesia was the 2005 Bali Interfaith Dialogue under the auspices of the Asia-Europe Meeting which aimed to build interfaith harmony in the international community.[486] Still some recognise that Indonesia has, namely with the conflict in West Papua, potential to integrate interfaith processes as a way to overcome some of the challenges inherent in the conflict.[487] Also evaluating the role of faith-based organisations that exist within Indonesia, there are ways that they can be improved to help assist in interfaith dialogue. Associations and networks between the various faith-based organisations can be strengthened where interfaith organisations can regularly engage to ensure they are most effectively delivering social services. This need became clear following the disaster relief efforts of the Aceh tsunami disaster in 2004 where partnerships would have been an effective way to enhance the interfaith cooperation and deliver the required services.[488]

Indeed, there are ways for Indonesia to enhance the effectiveness of its interfaith strategies. Critically, Kovacs suggests that since the Indonesian transition to democracy, conflicts fuelled by religion have become more visible and the state has been passive in adjusting structures that could abate these tensions.[489] Yet, the Indonesian case does highlight some critical conclusions. The outcomes of interfaith dialogue in Indonesia have been

485 See Florian Pohl, "On the Role of Interreligious Dialogue in Religious Studies Programs at Indonesian State Islamic Universities," *Journal of Ecumenical Studies* 50, no. 1 (2015): 162.

486 Republic of Indonesia Ministry of Foreign Affairs, "Bali Interfaith Dialogue" https://www.kemlu.go.id/en/berita/siaran-pers/Pages/Bali-Interfaith-Dialogue.aspx.

487 See Neles Tebay, "'Papua, the Land of Peace': The Interfaith Vision and Commitment for West Papua," *Exchange* 36, no. 4 (2007).

488 Sakai, "Building a Partnership for Social Service Delivery in Indonesia: State and Faith-Based Organisations," 384-385.

489 See Amanda Kovacs, "Indonesia's Religious Conflicts: Recent Developments, Causes and Policy Implications for Peace" *The German Journal on Contemporary Asia* 127 (2013).

influenced by a variety of different sources. One source, in fact, is from Islamic academia in the United States, where intellectuals derived theory from the Quran to develop a standard of ethics that solve contemporary social, political and economic problems evident in the case of Indonesia.[490] Examining the US case in the following section will help to assert why they have been so influential, even in Indonesia. Independently, however, Indonesia has projected itself as a leader in incorporating religious dialogue into post-conflict reconstruction and utilising policy strategically to enhance pluralism within a multi-religious society.

5 Interfaith Dialogue: the American Experience

As discussed earlier in this paper, many of the theoretical and foundational frameworks of interfaith dialogue emerged from the US, which has caused many to believe that the US has been the leader in the development of interfaith dialogue. After the dramatic events of 9/11, interfaith dialogue came quickly into the spotlight of global attention. Even as a result of the US involvement in the Middle East, interfaith dialogue has become a feature of many American policies. These programs, however, have not always yielded positive results, but they do demonstrate the opportunity present in incorporating interfaith programs within broader diplomatic strategy. Some observers regard the rising presence of interfaith organisations in the US as an 'interfaith movement' in which a network between interfaith groups has grown exponentially in recent years, with the Pluralism Project identifying that 80 per cent of groups believing that relationship building was their primary purpose, followed by education, dialogue, service and then spiritual development.[491] The interfaith work in the United States has developed into various forms over time, with grassroots projects, locally sponsored dialogues, national denominational bodies, and also federal faith-based initiatives all operating across the nation.[492]

Religious pluralism in the United States has been enshrined historically as a legal fact within the state as it underpins a free society. Religious pluralism is protected by Article VI of the American Constitution, and the American

490 Ahmad Najib Burhani, "Transmission of Islamic Reform from the United States to Indonesia," *Indonesia & the Malay World* 41, no. 119 (2013): 44.

491 Eck, "Interfaith Dialogue in the New Religious America," 29.

492 Brad Fulton and Richard L. Wood, "Interfaith Community Organizing Emerging Theological and Organizational Challenges," *International Journal of Public Theology* 6, no. 4 (2012): 398.

society continues to recognise the values of a religiously pluralistic society in different manifestations.[493] This has given rise to the notion that the US is a 'Christian nation,' with a majority of Americans believing that Christianity played a pivotal role in its founding yet studies contest the depth and reality of this perception.[494] The religious landscape within America has become increasingly diversified with religious freedom and immigration policies changing the nature of religious identities. Data has been produced that clarifies the religious landscape of the US, with some studies suggesting that Americans are gradually becoming less Christian, with a slowly diminishing dominance of the Christian majority in the country and many minority groups now having more access to the decision-making structures.[495] Of note in the data is a growing trend of negative public perceptions towards minority groups with respondents claiming that these minority religious groups were unlikely to represent core American values.[496] This suggests that being from a minority religious group is 'antithetical to being a good American' and has challenged the national idea.[497] Currently, religious authorities in America must be more engaged in countering religiously motivated violence primarily as it manifests as terrorism and protracted warfare. Danforth suggests that this can be achieved through interfaith initiatives and collaboration with the US State Department as they employ strategies in countries where religion is a present catalyst for political conflicts.[498] In fact, it is a consistent trend that formal dialogues between religious communities in the US have been pursued to foster positive relationships and collaborate on mutual issues. In this, minority religious communities require interfaith dialogue in America as a way of survival, and yet dominant religious groups know that dialogue is an integral part of addressing emerging social movements and contributing to justice.[499] A marked shift in the US' engagement with interfaith dialogue came as a result of 9/11.

493 J.E.W, "Interfaith Dialogue," 5.

494 Stephen M. Merino, "Religious Diversity in a "Christian Nation": The Effects of Theological Exclusivity and Interreligious Contact on the Acceptance of Religious Diversity," *Journal for the Scientific Study of Religion* 49, no. 2 (2010): 243-244.

495 McCormack, "Interfaith Relations in the United States: Toward a Multilevel Community Psychology Approach," 172-173.

496 Ibid., 172-173.

497 See Merino, "Religious Diversity in a "Christian Nation": The Effects of Theological Exclusivity and Interreligious Contact on the Acceptance of Religious Diversity," 233-243.

498 Danforth, "Mobilizing Religion against Terrorism," 77.

499 Tiemeier, "Interreligious Reading in the Context of Dialogue: When Interreligious Reading 'Fails'," 138.

The commentary and rhetoric surrounding the events of 9/11 did evoke tensions against Islamic communities, highlighted by President Bush's comments calling for what some observed as a 'Crusade against Muslims' all the while discontentment grew with wars in Iraq and Afghanistan.[500] These activities generated Islamophobia in the West and anti-Western sentiment in the Muslim world.[501] There were significant implications to this event that are still being felt in the international system.[502] Within America, however, Muslim communities immediately were confronted by mistrust, and to gain the acceptance of their neighbours, Muslims required activities and organisations that demonstrated high levels of forgiveness.[503] For the Muslim communities in America, there was an immediate need to engage with other groups to ensure that harmonious pluralism in the US could be managed, with Muslim groups calling for a recognition of America as their true homeland.[504] President Bush, during this time, began the Office of Faith-based and Community Initiatives as a way to increase partnerships between religious communities and the federal government, an office that was later reviewed and revised by the Obama administration.[505] The position of the US government needed to respond to the interfaith issues growing internally and internationally, and thus dialogue became a key feature of their policies in the post-9/11 environment.

Studies indicate that since 9/11, Christian and non-Christian groups in the United States have called for deeper and more sincere understandings and activities between faith groups with the number of interfaith groups rising, but their impact at the community level still being recognised.[506] Importantly, interfaith dialogue shifted in the wake of 9/11, as interactions between Muslim and Christian groups went from 'conversion of' to 'conversation with' the other party.[507] The reality of this environment in America is an increase in the awareness of religious diversity, particularly in reference to a growing Muslim population as part of a non-Christian presence, which has required groups to improve their knowledge and relationships with other religious

500 Ayoub, "9/11 and the Need for a New Paradigm for Interfaith Dialogue," 563.

501 Ibid., 563.

502 See Philpott, "The Challenge of September 11 to Secularism in International Relations."

503 Ayoub, "9/11 and the Need for a New Paradigm for Interfaith Dialogue," 563.

504 Liyakatali Takim, "From Conversion to Conversation: Interfaith Dialogue Inpost 9-11 America," ibid., 94 (2004): 343.

505 Christy Lohr Sapp, "Obama's Interfaith Service Challenge: A Call for a New Theology of Service in American Higher Education," *Dialog: A Journal of Theology* 50, no. 3 (2011): 282.

506 Todd, Houston-Kolnik, and Suffrin, "Understanding Community Issues of Interfaith Groups," 161.

507 Takim, "From Conversion to Conversation: Interfaith Dialogue Inpost 9-11 America," 345.

groups, hence why interfaith movements across the US have quantitatively increased.[508]

The most poignant affirmation of interfaith dialogue by any administration in the post-9/11 system came from President Obama's historic 'New Beginning' speech delivered at Cairo University on June 4, 2009.[509] The statement committed the United States to work with Muslim communities around the world from a 'new beginning' that was built on a shared commitment to tolerance, justice, progress and the dignity of humanity.[510] The statement was well-received by the international community and renewed the American engagement in interfaith activities. Beyond statements, however, President Obama also launched interfaith cooperation and community service campaigns, labelling them as a way to 'contribute to the common good.'[511] This was known as Obama's challenge to service, where he called on American colleges to design and implement interfaith community service projects.[512] The program was managed through the Office of Faith-based and Neighbourhood Partnerships and demonstrated a clear priority for interfaith cooperation under the Obama administration.[513] This shows the commitment of US leadership to engage with interfaith programs.

Another way that interfaith progress is manifesting in the US is through institution-based community organisations that bridge racial, class, religious and ideological fragmentations. The geographic reach of these organisations has extended to engage in new states and cities and are going beyond just local projects to engage with the state and national level, even though they are still limited by financial support.[514] Challenging this, however, are trends of religious identification in the US. These see that a growing number of the population have chosen to identify as non-religious, but even in these non-homogeneous groupings, many adherents maintain basic spiritual practices

508 Shoemaker and Edmonds, "The Limits of Interfaith? Interfaith Identities, Emerging Potentialities, and Exclusivity," 203.

509 For the full transcript see Barack Obama, "Remarks by the President on a New Beginning" https://obamawhitehouse.archives.gov/the-press-office/remarks-president-cairo-university-6-04-09.

510 Mandour, "Islam and Religious Freedom: Role of Interfaith Dialogue in Promoting Global Peace," 885.

511 Todd, Houston-Kolnik, and Suffrin, "Understanding Community Issues of Interfaith Groups," 161.

512 See Sapp, "Obama's Interfaith Service Challenge: A Call for a New Theology of Service in American Higher Education," 280-282.

513 Ibid., 282.

514 Fulton and Wood, "Interfaith Community Organizing Emerging Theological and Organizational Challenges," 399-401.

while choosing to reject the institutional manifestations of religion.[515] The most pressing challenge is that rising suspicion and anti-Islamic sentiment within the United States. This has bolstered the need for Muslim organisations to engage with mainstream politics and cultures with a resilience that actively responds to the issues in society.[516] As a result, there has been a strong focus on Muslim relations in the US.

A key point of analysis has been the way that the United States has been able to manage tensions and Islamophobia as growing discontent between the US and Islamic communities grew elsewhere in the world. Within America, Muslims see that Islam recognises ideals such as democracy and pluralism, and groups within the state have worked to reconcile these values with the communities. This has seen leaders attempt to "present the blending of Islamic values with the American experience as a solid bridge to mutual understanding between the United States and the Muslim world."[517] But the diversity of the Muslim community in America suggests that there is no single approach that can address all of the issues confronting the communities in America, whether it be based on human rights, religious intolerance, or even violence.[518] As Takim highlights, Muslim communities in the United States had to learn how to engage in interfaith dialogue, as their own countries never really had the need to converse with groups in this same way, which meant these religious groups required to learn the processes of interfaith dialogue very quickly in the shadow of great tension.[519]

As a way to curb the growing tension regarding terrorism around the world, the Fiqh Council of North America released a fatwa in 2005 that condemned acts of terrorism and religious extremism. The fatwa interpreted Islamic theology and doctrine to condemn religious extremism and terrorism highlighting that there is no justification in Islam for this to occur, including through suicide bombing or other terrorist attacks.[520] In fact, after the London bombings in July of 2005, a fatwa in the US poignantly asserted the Islamic perspective on the attacks stating that: (1) all acts of terrorism targeting civilians are

515 Shoemaker and Edmonds, "The Limits of Interfaith? Interfaith Identities, Emerging Potentialities, and Exclusivity," 208-209.

516 Qamar-Ul Huda, "Conflict Prevention and Peace-Building Efforts by American Muslim Organizations Following September 11," *Journal of Muslim Minority Affairs* 26, no. 2 (2006): 190.

517 Ibid., 187.

518 Ibid., 189.

519 Takim, "From Conversion to Conversation: Interfaith Dialogue Inpost 9-11 America," 345.

520 Huda, "Conflict Prevention and Peace-Building Efforts by American Muslim Organizations Following September 11," 190.

forbidden in Islam; (2) it is forbidden for a Muslim to cooperate with any individual or group involved in any act of terrorism or violence; and (3) it is the civic and religious duty of Muslims to cooperate with law enforcement authorities to protect the lives of all civilians.[521] This example shows how faith-based organisations can provide a poignant narrative to counter tensions in society that address and respond to specific issues around the world. These fatwas help to clarify the position of a community and provide a basis for understanding for adherents to other faiths and provide a strong basis for interfaith engagement.

Another challenge to the Muslim community in the United States is that the capacity for the community to engage actively in dialogue is regularly changing. Newer migrant groups arrive in America and the experiences of Islam as a result of 'imported Islam' are resistant to change. Thus, traditional norms are reaffirmed, and the new communities are hesitant to engage in interfaith dialogue.[522] Observing the Muslim organisations within the US, the main goal of interfaith dialogue is the belief "that building trust, peace, and reconciliation will lead to harmonious interfaith relations in the United States and ultimately in the Muslim world."[523] This recognises that what is done domestically has the ability to project into foreign policy and international perceptions of the US.

Looking toward specific examples, several interfaith dialogue groups exist within the United States, and many have been strengthened based on the needs in society responding to global events.[524] The Islamic Society of North America, for example, works in partnership with the National Muslim-Christian Initiative, engages with the organisation Children of Abraham: Jews and Muslims in Conversation, a group that works in partnership with the Union for Reform of Judaism.[525] These organisations suggest that a network exists between interfaith groups, recognising the need for a strong commitment to interfaith initiatives.

As many of the global initiatives of interfaith dialogue began out of the US, there is strong historical participation of interfaith programs. In light of the Vatican II declaration from the Catholic Church, the Catholic Archdiocese of Los Angeles participated in the Interreligious Council of Southern California

521 Ibid., 191.

522 Takim, "From Conversion to Conversation: Interfaith Dialogue Inpost 9-11 America," 350.

523 Huda, "Conflict Prevention and Peace-Building Efforts by American Muslim Organizations Following September 11," 187-188.

524 See Borelli, "Christian-Muslim Relations in the United States: Reflections for the Future after Two Decades of Experience," 323-326.

525 Discussed in Magonet, "The Growth of Interfaith Dialogue," 41-42.

in 1969 with bilateral interfaith dialogues emerging from this meeting.[526] An example of the expansion of interfaith meetings is the Catholic and Hindu dialogue that was established during this time but has continued on with the goals of: establishing a formal and ongoing dialogue, encouraging contact between Los Angeles' Hindu and Catholic religious communities, growing awareness of historical developments between these communities, identifying areas of mutual concern and, developing language and frameworks for exploration of religious topics and themes.[527]

From the Islamic perspective, a number of Muslim faith-based organisations have been established in the United States to contribute to areas of conflict resolution, dialogue, education, activism, human rights, and humanitarian activities, among others.[528] Muslim advocacy groups within America worked closely with government and law enforcement agencies to create strategies to address issues on public policy, rights, the war against terrorism and other pressing concerns within the state.[529]

An example of Muslim-Christian dialogue that occurred in the wake of 9/11 is the West Coast Dialogue of Catholics and Muslims, which worked together to generate points of consensus in their meetings through 2003. Some of these points include:

1. We (Catholics and Muslims) believe that God is the source of peace and justice, and thus we fundamentally agree on the nature of peace and justice and the essential need of all to work for peace and justice.
2. Our rich teachings and traditions of peace and justice serve as a resource and inspiration for all; however, our immediate and present actions to work together are often wanting. The need to work together for peace and justice is a pressing demand in these troubled times.
3. We believe that it is God who forgives and that as Catholics and Muslims we are called by God to offer forgiveness. Forgiveness is an important step to moving beyond our past history if we are to preserve human dignity, to effect justice, and to work for peace.
4. We may disagree on certain points of doctrine, even as we respect the others' rights to believe in the fundamental integrity of their teachings and affirm all their human and religious rights. With love and in the pursuit of truth, we will offer our criticisms of one another when we believe

526 Tiemeier, "Interreligious Reading in the Context of Dialogue: When Interreligious Reading 'Fails'," 139-141.

527 Ibid., 141.

528 For examples of specific organisations, see Huda, "Conflict Prevention and Peace-Building Efforts by American Muslim Organizations Following September 11," 192-200.

529 Ibid., 187.

there is a violation of integrity of faith in God. We must avoid demonizing one another and misrepresenting on another's teachings and traditions.

5. When we meet in dialogue and discuss matters of peace, justice, and forgiveness, while being faithful to our traditions, we have experienced a profound and moving connection on the deepest level of our faith, which must take effect in our lives.[530]

These areas of agreement are a clear picture of how interfaith dialogue can effectively provide a response to global issues and find common interests that are complementary to the principles and goals of conflict resolution and diplomacy.

Eck observes that a number of interfaith initiatives in the US are focused locally. She also highlights that there has been a concerted effort for these local interfaith initiatives to engage with women.[531] This does not mean that national campaigns are ignored, but rather several institutions work within a national umbrella structure that focuses organisations on fulfilling a specific purpose within society, such as the Interfaith Worker Justice which advocates for workers and wages or the Interfaith Youth Corps which highlights youth service initiatives.[532] These grassroots initiatives have the ability to more adequately address communal tension and public perceptions. For example, to directly address the issue of Islamophobia, Osborn assessing the work of certain interfaith organisations 'Shoulder to Shoulder with American Muslims' to highlight how this interfaith group is targeting specific issues within American society.[533] As alluded to earlier, however, the policies of interfaith dialogue within the US have been informed by the US policies abroad. In fact, the US foreign policies have been a source of discontent for communities within the US and therein lies a unique challenge for the US. They must balance their global influence and policies abroad, with particular attention paid to interfaith issues, to ensure that there is stability internally in the same area.

Following the events of 9/11, American Muslims became key stakeholders in providing information and consultation for US foreign policy decisions, namely towards the wars in Iraq and Afghanistan.[534] Muslim organisations in

530 Borelli, "Christian-Muslim Relations in the United States: Reflections for the Future after Two Decades of Experience," 332-333.

531 See Eck, "Interfaith Dialogue in the New Religious America," 29-30.

532 Ibid., 29-30.

533 See Catherine Orsborn, "Shoulder to Shoulder with American Muslims: What the Interreligious Community Is Doing to Combat Anti-Muslim Bigotry in America," *Journal of Ecumenical Studies* 51, no. 2 (2016).

534 Huda, "Conflict Prevention and Peace-Building Efforts by American Muslim Organizations Following September 11," 188.

America not only provide policy analysis, but some have worked closely with law enforcement officials to identify instances of intolerance that might arise as a result of this closer linkage.[535] Danforth outlines the ways in which the US government has engaged in interfaith activities, demonstrating the commitment of multiple administrations to interfaith programs. Working within the State Department, several programs have been initiated to engage with religious leaders and promote interfaith dialogue as a conducive avenue for conflict mitigation.[536] Within the government structures, Secretary of State John Kerry created the Office of Religion and Global Affairs in 2013, and while budgetary restrictions and vacancy of key positions are putting the Office's role in doubt in the Trump administration, the Office has been a valuable tool of religious engagement through embassies and outposts around the world.[537] While the US government cannot do the work of the religious leaders, it can facilitate interfaith dialogue among leaders at the embassy level. An interesting challenge in this regard is that interfaith movements have had to contend with the Western and colonial perception that is attached to US policies internationally. Thus, US policies of interfaith movements will need to consider the best formation of interfaith dialogue across borders and anticipate what this might look like in the future.[538]

The US interfaith experience has not always been positive in the post-9/11 international system. Even though the policymakers in the United States have recognised the need to address their image abroad, particularly the anti-American sentiment prevalent in the Middle East, strategies have not fully penetrated those societies. To best explore the American policies to improve their image abroad, the lens of public diplomacy will be applied. It is out of the scope of this paper to fully explore the theory of public diplomacy, but to provide a simple definition, it is a "government's process of communicating with foreign publics in an attempt to bring about understanding for its nation's ideas and ideals, its institutions and cultures, as well as its national goals and current policies."[539] Some critique public diplomacy and argue that it is a form of public relations that seeks to maintain and manage images abroad.[540]

535 Ibid., 188.

536 The author offers the example as the Special Envoy for Peace in Sudan, see Danforth, "Mobilizing Religion against Terrorism," 83-84.

537 Ibid., 83-84.

538 Shoemaker and Edmonds, "The Limits of Interfaith? Interfaith Identities, Emerging Potentialities, and Exclusivity," 211.

539 Touch cited in M.J. Dutta-Bergman, "U.S. Public Diplomacy in the Middle East: A Critical Cultural Approach," *Journal of Communication Inquiry* 30, no. 2 (2006).

540 Ibid., 103.

Within these basic definitions, it is evident that religion plays a vital role in defining a people's ideals, cultures and institutions. Thus, to effectively maintain perception and national image, there is reason to consider faith within the public diplomacy paradigm.

Following 9/11, global attention was cast on the Middle East and with the ongoing conflicts in Iraq and Afghanistan, public diplomacy measures were reinvigorated by the US as the predominant public diplomacy actor in the region.[541] President Bush had demanded that governments around the world support the US efforts in the Middle East following 9/11, strongly expressing that those who did not support the US were actively fighting against them, thus unnerving US allies in the Middle East who had actively been working against terrorism for some time.[542] The rhetoric and policies enacted by the US increased a perception in the Middle East that the US was deliberately targeting Muslims. Phrases were used that evoked the imagery of the crusades of Christians fighting against Islam, and although efforts were put in place to mitigate these concerns, such as Bush's declaration that terror was not the true face of Islam, the message had already stirred up tension.[543] The US had to respond quickly to these claims to ensure that the cultural and religious divides swelling domestically and internationally did not escalate to conflict. A number of key strategies were conducted to manage this issue, including the creation of the Office of Global Communications which aimed to gain favour in the sight of the Middle East public, with websites, advertisements, news stories and radio programs being used to improve the image of the US government.[544]

These activities sought to address the anti-American sentiment with broadcasting and outreach efforts from the government to Arab audiences, with the logic of these programs being that the US policies have been miscommunicated or perceived incorrectly, yet these policies were disregarded as the media channels in the Middle East poignantly countered the American message.[545] Whether the policies were flawed or miscommunicated, the US government

541 L. Khatib, "Public Diplomacy in the Middle East: Dynamics of Success and Failure," *Diplomatic Studies* 6 (2011): 133.

542 William A. Rugh, *American Encounters with Arabs the "Soft Power" of U.S. Public Diplomacy in the Middle East* (Westport, Conn.: Praeger Security International, 2006), 152.

543 Ibid., 156.

544 Dutta-Bergman, "U.S. Public Diplomacy in the Middle East: A Critical Cultural Approach," 102.

545 Erik C. Nisbet and Teresa A. Myers, "Anti-American Sentiment as a Media Effect? Arab Media, Political Identity, and Public Opinion in the Middle East," *Communication Research* 38, no. 5 (2011): 685.

began to critically focus on a process of 'strategic communication' that engaged specific audiences to create conditions favourable to the US objectives.[546] To turn the tide of perception, using this strategic communication approach, government policies and messaged became centred on culture – the American values and ideals – as opposed to persuasion or propaganda.[547]

It was at this point that religion could be brought into the scope of strategies employed in the Middle East, and yet there was a detrimental inattention of religion in the policy objectives.[548] Fabrycky notes that the US is uniquely positioned to project religion positively in the Middle East as the American religiosity is apparent in their history, and yet blends with political modernism and societal conservatism that may seem attractive to many Muslim communities.[549] To present these, US public diplomacy had to promote that the US is interested in the values important to Islamic communities and actively listen to the communities in interfaith dialogue.[550]

Focusing specifically on the public diplomacy strategies utilised by the US government, an Undersecretary of State for Public Diplomacy and Public Affairs position was created. To the detriment of the position's legitimacy, it was filled by a number of different people through this critical time. Each undersecretary employed various strategies to address the issues in the Middle East and some will be drawn out here to present how the US utilised public diplomacy strategies with an interfaith element. Charlotte Beers held the position from 2001-2003 and utilised her advertising background to 'brand' the American image and values abroad.[551] She invested in a 'Muslims in America' campaign which featured domestically and on foreign television, and in print format, where small documentaries showed Muslims living in America sharing each other's values. While this was designed to change perceptions in foreign publics, Arab governments refused to show the ads as they did not want to be perceived as positively endorsing the United States. Beers also published an Arabic magazine called 'Hi' which sought to engage with younger generations to again promote shared values. These early examples demonstrate the

546 Michael H. Creswell, "Wasted Words? The Limitations of U.S. Strategic Communication and Public Diplomacy," *Studies in Conflict & Terrorism* (2017): 1-2.

547 Dutta-Bergman, "U.S. Public Diplomacy in the Middle East: A Critical Cultural Approach," 121-122.

548 David Fabrycky, "U.S. Public Diplomacy and Religion in the Muslim World," *The Review of Faith & International Affairs* 3, no. 2 (2005): 28-29.

549 Ibid., 28-29.

550 Ibid., 28-29.

551 Rugh, *American Encounters with Arabs the "Soft Power" of U.S. Public Diplomacy in the Middle East*. 157-160.

attempts of the US at addressing issues of perception and tension, but they did not effectively deal with the deeper divides that had become apparent in society. In 2003 Margaret Tutwiler took the post but only remained in the post for one year. In 2005 Karen Hughes was appointed to the position and worked to build on earlier public diplomacy campaigns, but the changes hindered a consistent message being promoted.[552] Public diplomacy policies changed their focus in 2004 to start engaging with exchange programs, such as the Youth Exchange and Study program, which allowed Muslim teenagers to study in the United States in hopes that the exchange experience would challenge misconceptions between audiences.[553] The programs rightly identified significant issues that were apparent in the Middle East, and used a public diplomacy approach to address these concerns, but they were limited in their success.

Khatib explores these limitations and states that the US public diplomacy strategy did not fully explain their policy, did not provide alternative and factual sources of information to enhance the credibility of their message to local audiences, and they struggled to effectively project the core values that characterise American society.[554] American public diplomacy initiatives began to recognise that these three components were lacking, and started to work with broadcasting programs in the Middle East to promote values such as freedom and democracy while ensuring the message was supported by credible news sources within the region.[555] The concern with this values-based approach to the American public diplomacy strategies was that there is often a disconnect between the ideal values and the experienced values on the ground with the American foreign policy decisions, namely in Afghanistan and Iraq, and even domestic concerns, such as Guantanamo detentions, visa restrictions, and growing divisions between Muslim and non-Muslim populations within America, all delegitimising the public diplomacy policies abroad.[556]

To improve the effectiveness of public diplomacy strategies in the Middle East, some recommendations have been offered by observers. Interestingly, these recommendations illuminate a space for more concerted interfaith programs to be performed. Douglas and Neal proposed six recommendations after

552 Ibid., 148.

553 Ibid., 157-156.

554 Khatib, "Public Diplomacy in the Middle East: Dynamics of Success and Failure," 140.

555 Ibid., 141.

556 Ibid., 143-144.

their report on public diplomacy in the Muslim world following 9/11. Their six recommendations include:

1. Defining the goals of the program. In Muslim-majority countries, the US aims to influence attitudes and behaviours in a way that goes beyond just protecting their reputation. America's story can be told, and changing attitudes and behaviours is also a valuable goal, but those goals must be balanced and defined in programs.
2. Listening is an integral part of engaging with diverse Muslim societies. Understanding language and concerns develops credibility and mutual understanding between parties, and this avenue of listening must be made available.
3. Measuring the success of the programs can help identify what strategies deserve long-term investment and support. Parties in the US lack clear information on how the public diplomacy strategies in Muslim-majority countries are working which means less chance of support from agencies.
4. Ensure that programs are designed to reach their target audience. There are important differences between countries and even within countries, so those initiating public diplomacy strategies must clearly define their target audience through clear understanding of the demography in the region.
5. Exchange people and ideas. The branding and projection of a certain message is one element of public diplomacy, but the full extent of public diplomacy can be felt through exchange. Fulbright scholarships, for example, are ways to ensure exposure to opportunities to clarify misunderstandings between cultures and values.
6. Finally, get outside the bubble of official agencies and embassies to engage with innovative outreach programs to expand the policies and opportunities available.[557]

With particular reference to incorporating religion more effectively in the US public diplomacy strategy, Fabrycky provides several points of discussion that were not realised in strategy and thus did not fully engage with the interfaith element of this situation. First, Muslim publics abroad need to be made more aware of the Muslim-American communities within the US. Once Muslims have experienced the American society, they generally leave exchange opportunities with a more positive perception of the US. There are also government programs which focus on reforming political, economic and human rights

557 Walter Douglas and Jeanne Neal, *Engaging the Muslim World Public Diplomacy after 9/11 in the Arab Middle East, Afghanistan, and Pakistan* (Lanham: Center for Strategic & International Studies, 2013), 7-8.

issues in the Middle East, but could incorporate religious leaders and religious communities more closely to engage in transforming the society. There has also been a call for the US government to incorporate more Muslim-Americans into decision-making roles and see channels for American Muslim communities to engage with policy considerations and strategies. Furthermore, Muslim communities around the world will generally respond to US strategies with mistrust as it can be viewed as an attempt to 'Americanize Islam' so the US must keep a keen focus on credibility. Finally, US policies should be context-specific and highlight the needs and interests of the community with which they engage, ensuring that there is a more long-term approach to policies that engage with religion.[558]

The analysis of public diplomacy efforts by the United States toward the Middle East demonstrates that the US recognised the need to address the perception of the US abroad. They also noted an increasing divide between the Arab world and the US which had domestic and international implications. However, strategies to address these areas of communication were relatively tokenistic and lacked the credibility in terms of the values presented and the experience on the ground. Furthermore, while the Muslim attitudes were reflected in some policies, there was the need for deeper engagement with religion, and programs of an interfaith nature, in conjunction with broader public diplomacy strategies, could have enhanced the effectiveness of the US policies in the Middle East.

Looking more broadly now at recommendations for domestic and international interfaith programs in the US, some recommendations can be offered that are applicable in the US context. After several years representing the United States Conference of Catholic Bishops, Borelli offers ten lessons that he discovered through interfaith dialogue to improve the Christian-Muslim interactions in the United States. A brief summary of these lessons include: (1) Muslims feel compelled to teach Christians the basic foundations of Islam as there are many prevalent misconceptions about Islamic theology; (2) Muslims often speak in generalities with other religious groups; (3) although Christians and Muslims share many expressions, there are subtle nuances that vary the meanings of these terms within their contexts; (4) Muslims often regard Christianity as one group and do not understand how if one Christian has a different perspective on theology or belief, they are not necessarily disassociated with another group; (5) Muslims expect Christians to live a similar moral life as there are consistent moral principles evident in the Abrahamic traditions; (6) Muslims are eager to explain their respect for Jesus to Christians;

558 Fabrycky, "U.S. Public Diplomacy and Religion in the Muslim World," 28-29.

(7) the concept of 'mission' in Christian circles actually holds similar meaning to the Islamic concept of 'jihad' and this misinterpretation can be corrected; (8) Christianity is a highly structured religion which may require some explanation; (9) Muslims and Christians can find areas of common ground in the way they share their everyday experiences, and; (10) Christians and Muslims often judge the other group by the extremists who argue they represent their traditions.[559] These lessons reveal the common misconceptions held between religious traditions in the United States and show that interfaith programs can go a long way in clarifying these concerns, translating in mutual understanding and respect in society as a counter to misunderstandings and tension. As a key issue in the US is the management of the relationship between Muslim and non-Muslim groups, these lessons provide valuable guidance on how strategies can be strengthened in the future.

Beyond the Muslim-Christian relations in the US, Eck recommends developing an 'interfaith infrastructure' where the complex geography of cities and suburbs have access to interfaith activities and civic engagement at various levels, including nationally, to promote a common society to all American citizens.[560] The proper support and funding of faith-based community organisations can continue the progress made by these institutions in the US to build bridges between what can often be exclusive congregational life and working within the community.[561] This is an effective form of interfaith engagement which requires dialogue to form and can be an open door to engage in future dialogue.

In terms of research, there is still much to be done to confidentially address the interfaith challenges in the US. Merino notes that there is no clear consensus about the place that non-Christian perspectives have in American society and that more generally Americans are divided on how to engage with non-Christian positions.[562] This type of division is where interfaith dialogue can play a clear role.

What the US case highlights is that interfaith dialogue is effective when targeting specific issues. However, the legitimacy and credibility of interfaith programs can be undermined internally if foreign policy decisions are not made effectively. While there has been some success in the US experience

559 For the full explanation of each of these points, see Borelli, "Christian-Muslim Relations in the United States: Reflections for the Future after Two Decades of Experience," 326-327.

560 Eck, "Interfaith Dialogue in the New Religious America," 30.

561 Fulton and Wood, "Interfaith Community Organizing Emerging Theological and Organizational Challenges," 420.

562 Merino, "Religious Diversity in a 'Christian Nation': The Effects of Theological Exclusivity and Interreligious Contact on the Acceptance of Religious Diversity," 244-245.

of interfaith dialogue, they have not always achieved their desired goals. The public diplomacy strategies of the US in the Middle East post-9/11 clearly indicate that while interfaith issues were recognised, they were not adequately defined and addressed. This suggests that there is potential for US diplomacy to improve their interfaith capacities. That has not, however, stopped the US from pursuing programs and initiatives domestically to ensure that interfaith tensions are managed. The US have historically been a leader in the development of interfaith strategies and have the capacity to do so if faith becomes a more integral component of diplomatic strategies in the future.

6 Conclusions

The contemporary international system has seen a resurgence of religion in the issues of global affairs. Religious traditions and faith groups have traversed traditional borders as a result of globalisation. With that movement have come a myriad of issues that governments must manage, however, due to the separation of church and state evident in the structures of governance, this has been a challenge. As a result, new perspectives on peacemaking, policy construction and diplomacy are required to engage with these emergent challenges. Terrorist acts committed in the name of religion, religiously motivated violence, identity-based conflict and social disharmony due to the marginalisation of groups are all unfortunate features of the 21st century, reinforcing the need for a deeper appreciation of faith in policy.

The emergence of faith-based diplomacy as an approach to diplomatic practice has been gaining momentum in recent decades. Since its inception in scholarship in 1994, scholars and practitioners have sought to incorporate religious considerations into peacemaking and diplomacy to address contemporary challenges. This has resulted in a number of frameworks for countering extremism, establishing post-conflict rebuilding and inspiring reconciliation. At the diplomatic level, faith-based diplomacy has advocated for the inclusion of grassroots organisations and religious leaders at various levels of diplomatic engagement, including as third-party mediators in conflict negotiations. While faith-based diplomacy is still conceptually new to the field of International Relations, it has filled a gap in scholarship and practice. Essentially, as religion and faith were considered as internal, structures of governance and conflict resolution did not adequately address the tensions that arise from these concerns. Diplomatic mechanisms attempted to adjust their traditional frames of analysis, but this approach does not effectively manage the root causes of conflict. With a number of scholars and practitioners developing frames of analysis and methods of diplomacy from a faith-based perspective, this area of diplomacy has the potential to expand and be integrated more meaningfully into diplomatic strategy.

While violence stemming from religious motivations is understood, history also presents cases of conflict between religious groups. As a result, interfaith dialogue has been utilised as a strategy for mitigating tension between different religious groups. Typically, this process has been developed within different fields, but has not yet been fully recognised within the scope of diplomacy. This is a major limitation for the advancement of faith-based diplomacy as interfaith dialogue has several natural complementarities, as discussed through this paper. After evaluating the methods, characteristics and opportunities of interfaith dialogue, it is evident that interfaith dialogue can be a useful process within strategies of faith-based diplomacy.

Interfaith dialogue has often been used as a response to events of religious tension. The prime example is how interfaith programs intensified in the US following 9/11. Over time the processes and aims of interfaith dialogue have evolved, with the central goals of interfaith dialogue now focusing on achieving tolerance, enhancing pluralism, developing mutual understanding, and sharing in genuine exchange. These goals can be reached through a variety of different methods, which have been tested over time and are continuing to mature in light of growth in the field. One such example of this growth is the way that Muslim perspectives of interfaith dialogue are being promoted to balance the historical Western dominance in the area. Observers have recognised a number of ways that interfaith dialogue can be improved in practice, but these recommendations serve to strengthen what is a valuable approach to addressing religious concerns.

While, in practice, the content of interfaith dialogue often focuses on discussions of theology, several states have found success in incorporating interfaith dialogue into their policies. Highlighted through this paper was the case of Indonesia, a state whose political philosophy of Pancasila girded interfaith processes in the community to affirm the value of pluralism and democracy. Not only did the state use interfaith dialogue as a way to build their societal culture and encourage harmony in a multi-religious society, but Indonesia also utilised interfaith dialogue as a tool of conflict resolution. Following significant conflicts between religious groups in Maluku in particular, Indonesian peacemakers engaged in a number of interfaith efforts involving participants from various sectors. What the Indonesian case reveals is that interfaith dialogue can provide resources for supporting characteristics such as pluralism and democracy but can also be effective in moving groups toward peace when communal issues are specified as goals within dialogue.

The experiences of interfaith dialogue from the United States also present some valuable conclusions. The theory and practice of interfaith dialogue historically have been associated with the United States. Policies and programs involving interfaith elements have been a key feature of US practice in response to religious tensions and developing social cohesion in a multi-religious society. The state has effectively employed interfaith strategies in response to events, such as the surge of interfaith programs following 9/11. Indeed, the United States has allowed government structures to engage with issues of religion to varying levels of success. While the domestic environment for interfaith dialogue has been relatively positive, challenges do still remain, including anti-Islamic sentiment and discontent toward migration issues. A number of interfaith programs are in operation to manage these issues, but the success of domestic activities has often been overshadowed by the US' inability to balance religious considerations in their foreign policy. By applying the lens of public diplomacy, this paper has found that the US identified interfaith issues but were unable to employ practical strategies that addressed interfaith tension in a timely manner. This does not suggest, however, that the US fails as an active participant and leader of interfaith dialogue, but it does recognise areas of improvement required to see religious concerns managed in this contemporary environment.

The purpose of this paper was to highlight the value of incorporating faith into diplomacy, noting the growth and development of the theories and practice of faith-based diplomacy. This perspective has the potential to address identity-based conflict, religious extremism, terrorism, reconciliation and support diplomatic processes by incorporating the positive assets of religion into decision-making. Another purpose of this paper was to examine interfaith dialogue and suggest that it is an appropriate time to incorporate interfaith dialogue more intentionally into diplomatic strategy. The nature of interfaith dialogue in the current international system must be improved to address religious concerns. Namely, interfaith dialogue must go beyond trying to manufacture tolerance and work toward genuine exchange. As a result of globalisation and multi-religious societies, interfaith dialogue should also see pluralism as a central goal. In practice, interfaith dialogue will be most valuable if it seeks to go beyond theological discussion and generate specific strategies to bring resolution to community issues. Working within a diplomatic strategy, primarily through faith-based diplomacy, interfaith dialogue has the potential to be a valuable resource at the diplomat's disposal. Incorporating faith and religion into diplomatic decision-making is an important perspective that, given the issues in the current international system, will strengthen the practice and scholarship of diplomacy.

6.1 *Limitations and Opportunities*

To conclude this paper, the challenges, limitation and competing explanations to faith-based approaches to diplomacy will be discussed. These considerations are important as they highlight the unique value of faith-based diplomacy and interfaith dialogue. Identifying the limitations and possible counter-explanations also ensure that if faith-based initiatives are incorporated into diplomatic strategy in the future, it will be done in the most effective way possible. Once these limitations have been discussed, the opportunities for future research in the field will be proposed to recommend to policymakers and theorists how to further investigate religious considerations to diplomacy.

One of the most substantial counter-explanations to the successes of faith-based diplomacy or interfaith dialogue is perceiving faith-based approaches to diplomacy as interest group politics. Within this paradigm, groups defined by common interests engage in diplomacy to achieve desired goals. Simply, religion would be the interest that define these groups. While this may work as a simplified categorisation, it does not fully appreciate the depth to which religion informs identity and motivates behaviour. The methods of diplomacy used by faith-based actors may be categorised as the way in which an interest group works to achieve their goals. However, the scope of faith-based diplomacy or interfaith dialogue goes beyond this pragmatic sense. The diplomacy of faith-based groups is not just attaining goals that satisfy immediate interests, but are rather, among others, the harmonisation of identity, the enhancing of social cohesion, the promotion of communal reconciliation. As religion is such a powerful component of identity, and also such a significant force in motivating behaviour, a specific strategy that targets those elements of society should be more effective in its impact. By extension, faith-based diplomacy and interfaith dialogue could be argued as part of identity politics.[563] Within this scope, religious groups are an important consideration. This conceptualisation does give weight to the identity-based issues inherent in faith groups, but often does not have targeted strategies that inform how these issues may be addressed diplomatically. Take, for example, the growing trend of identity-based conflicts as discussed earlier in this paper. Knowing that these conflicts were rising in frequency, and the mechanisms of conflict resolution were failing to address them, the theories of faith-based diplomacy were introduced to better address these concerns. Faith-based diplomacy and interfaith dialogue provide precise mechanisms for managing the manifest issues of identity politics. Faith-based diplomacy and interfaith dialogue also play a vital

563 For defining features of identity politics, see Mary Bernstein, "Identity Politics," *Annual Review of Sociology* 31 (2005).

clarifying role in the issues of identity and interest group politics. The incorporation of religious actors and principles in the diplomatic process elucidates the complexity associated with religion in politics. The fact that faith-based approaches provide a more targeted array of strategies that address specific issues validates further study in this area.

This is not to say, however, that faith-based diplomacy or interfaith dialogue are a panacea to all the religious troubles in the world. Used incorrectly, incorporating faith into practice may actually exacerbate tensions and intensify conflict. Including inappropriate actors and institutions may delegitimise the diplomatic process and tarnish the credibility of outcomes. This is why Albright warns that the purpose of faith-based diplomacy is not to replace traditional diplomacy.[564] Instead of replacing the traditional methods and actors of diplomacy, faith-based diplomacy seeks to provide more options and strategies to target religious issues as they may arise. Bercovitch notes that faith-based mediation is most successful when it works in tandem with traditional mediation.[565] Johnston recognises that faith-based diplomacy is valuable as it gives a frame for 'passing the baton' between faith-based actors and traditional diplomatic actors.[566] The purpose of this perspective of diplomacy is to recognise the importance of faith in the international system and provide tools for diplomatic actors to use to enhance diplomacy's effectiveness. In this paper, one such tool investigated was interfaith dialogue.

Given that the central premise of this paper was to provide analysis for faith-based diplomacy and examine the potentialities of interfaith dialogue as part of diplomatic strategy, there are a number of recommendations that may be useful for policy makers when conducting research in this area in the future. The first is that observers should continue to pay keen attention to the rising influence of religion in societies around the world. Whether this leads to the fragmentation of state authority, the politicisation of religion, or the hybridisation of religion in the public sphere, diplomacy can play a key role in mediating the engagement of a number of actors, including religious actors. By improving the structures and mechanisms of diplomacy to facilitate this participation, there can be a renewed legitimacy of diplomacy, from the state as well as from nonstate actors, in relevant communities.

564 Albright, "Faith and Diplomacy," 9.

565 See Bercovitch and Kadayifci-Orellana, "Religion and Mediation: The Role of Faith-Based Actors in International Conflict Resolution."

566 See Johnston, "Looking Ahead: Toward a New Paradigm." And Johnston, "Religion and Foreign Policy."

The trends of religion's growing importance are also being felt in research. Not only is the interest in faith-based diplomacy and interfaith dialogue indicative of that, but the growing research agenda within these areas suggests that there are significant opportunities to be pursued. One such opportunity is in using the current frameworks of faith-based diplomacy and applying them to a variety of different religious perspectives. As the study in the field has come from a Western-dominated position, the perspectives of other religious traditions and contexts will strengthen the research. In the same way that different religious perspectives can be applied to the frames of faith-based approaches to diplomacy, the existing frames can be applied to a variety of different cases. Different examples of conflicts and regions can continue to fortify the gains made in this area of study. Along with this, the increasing interdisciplinary focus afforded to faith-based diplomacy can increase the scholarly participation in the area. As mentioned in this paper, psychology, sociology, management, conflict resolution, negotiation, mediation and education are some of the research areas that have begun integrating faith-based and interfaith practices into their processes. Researchers can work to invite greater participation from these other disciplines to enhance the scope of faith-based diplomacy.

The methods available to diplomats seeking to integrate a faith-based approach should continue to be tested and developed. Practices, including programs like third-party mediation, educational programs, research conferences, or dialogues, will naturally expand as more policymakers engage in the process. This paper has sought to build on this point, highlighting interfaith dialogue as a program available for diplomats to consider in their strategies in the future. Seeing the value of this approach as a diplomatic practice will enable decisionmakers with more possibilities when addressing challenges of a religious nature.

At the introduction of this paper, it was established that this paper had two purposes. The first was to present faith-based diplomacy as an important perspective to be developed in contemporary Diplomacy Studies. By presenting the theoretical foundations and areas of practice in faith-based diplomacy, its value in the current international environment is apparent. With religion rising in influence around the world, and many of the world's conflicts being identity-based, the need for developing faith-based diplomacy is integral. The second central purpose of this paper was to propose interfaith dialogue as a viable framework to bring into the practice of faith-based diplomacy. By detailing the history, available methods, strengths and limitations of interfaith dialogue, this paper has found several complementarities between faith-based diplomacy and interfaith dialogue. The case analysis of interfaith dialogue strategies in both Indonesia and the United States have demonstrated the viability of interfaith dialogue as a part of diplomatic strategies. Incorporating considerations of faith into the theory and practice of diplomacy, namely through faith-based diplomacy and interfaith dialogue, is a valuable perspective of diplomacy and foreign policy that will assist in facing the challenges in the contemporary international system.

List of References

Abu-Nimer, Mohammed. "Religious Leaders in the Israeli-Palestinian Conflict: From Violent Incitement to Nonviolence Resistance." *Peace & Change* 36, no. 4 (2011): 556-80.

Agensky, Jonathan C. "Recognizing Religion: Politics, History, and the 'Long 19th Century'." *European Journal of International Relations* 23, no. 4 (2017): 729-55.

Aihiokhai, SimonMary Asese. "Going Beyond Nostra Aetate: The Way Forward for Interreligious Dialogue." *Journal of Ecumenical Studies* 51, no. 3 (2016): 386-401.

Aihiokhai, SimonMary Asese. "'Love One Another as I Have Loved You': The Place of Friendship in Interfaith Dialogue." 491-508: University of Pennsylvania Press, 2013.

Al Qurtuby, Sumanto. "Peacebuilding in Indonesia: Christian–Muslim Alliances in Ambon Island." *Islam and Christian–Muslim Relations* 24, no. 3 (2013): 1-19.

Al Qurtuby, Sumanto. "Religious Women for Peace and Reconciliation in Contemporary Indonesia." *International Journal on World Peace* 31, no. 1 (2014): 27-58.

Albright, Madelaine. "Faith and Diplomacy." *Review of Faith & International Affairs* 4, no. 2 (2006): 3-9.

Ali-Dib, Edith Szanto. "Inter-Religious Dialogue in Syria: Politics, Ethics and Miscommunication." *Political Theology* 9, no. 1 (2008): 93-113.

Ali, Muhamad. "'They Are Not All Alike'." *Indonesia & the Malay World* 38, no. 112 (2010): 329-47.

Ali, Muhammad Modassir. "A Muslim Interfaith Initiative (a Common Word between Us and You) and Its Christian Response." *Insights* 2, no. 1 (2009): 115-54.

Appleby, R. Scott. "Retrieving the Missing Dimension of Statecraft: Religious Faith in the Service of Peacebuilding." Chap. 9 In *Faith-Based Diplomacy: Trumping Realpolitik*, edited by Douglas M. Johnston, 231-58. New York: Oxford University Press, 2003.

Argon, Kemal. "Strategies for Interreligious and Inter-Muslim Dialogue: A Proposed Methodology." *Journal of Muslim Minority Affairs* 29, no. 3 (2009): 355-67.

Ariel, Yaakov. "Interfaith Dialogue and the Golden Age of Christian-Jewish Relations." 2010.

Ayoub, Mahmoud. "9/11 and the Need for a New Paradigm for Interfaith Dialogue." *Muslim World* 101, no. 3 (2011): 562-64.

Backues, Lindy. "Interfaith Development Efforts as Means to Peace and Witness." *Transformation: An International Journal of Holistic Mission Studies* 26, no. 2 (2009): 67-81.

Bakker, Freek L. "Inter-Religious Dialogue and Migrants the Case of the Netherlands." *Mission Studies: Journal of the International Association for Mission Studies* 31, no. 2 (2014): 227-54.

Baum, Gregory. "Interreligious Dialogue Includes Listening to Secular Voices." *Toronto Journal of Theology* 32, no. 2 (2016): 363-68.

Bercovitch, Jacob, and Ayse S. Kadayifci-Orellana. "Religion and Mediation: The Role of Faith-Based Actors in International Conflict Resolution." *International Negotiation* 14, no. 1 (2009): 175-204.

Beriker, Nimet. "The Conflict Resolution Field: Reflections on Multiple Realities, Challenges, and Geographical Divides." 7-22: Brown University, 2015.

Bernstein, Mary. "Identity Politics." *Annual Review of Sociology* 31 (2005): 47-74.

Beyer, Peter, and Lori G. Beaman. *Religion, Globalization and Culture*. Leiden, Boston: Brill, 2007.

Bolewski, Wilfried. "Corporate Diplomacy as Global Management." *International Journal of Diplomacy and Economy* 4, no. 2 (2018): 107-38.

Borelli, John. "Christian-Muslim Relations in the United States: Reflections for the Future after Two Decades of Experience." *Muslim World* 94, no. 3 (2004): 321-33.

Bretherton, Luke. "A Postsecular Politics? Inter-Faith Relations as a Civic Practice." *Journal of the American Academy of Religion* 79, no. 2 (2011): 346-77.

Brewer, John D., Gareth I. Higgins, and Francis Teeney. "Religion and Peacemaking: A Conceptualization." *Sociology* 44, no. 6 (2010): 1019-37.

Burhani, Ahmad Najib. "Transmission of Islamic Reform from the United States to Indonesia." *Indonesia & the Malay World* 41, no. 119 (2013): 29-47.

Burnett, Stanton. "Implications for the Foreign Policy Community." Chap. 13 In *Religion, the Missing Dimension of Statecraft*, edited by Douglas Johnston & Cynthia Sampson, 285-305. New York: Oxford University Press, 1994.

Burrell, David B. "Christian-Muslim Dialogue in a World Gone Religiously Awry." *Muslim World* 100, no. 4 (2010): 414-23.

Burrell, David B. "Some Requisites for Interfaith Dialogue." *New Blackfriars* 89, no. 1021 (2008): 300-10.

Cantle, Ted. "Parallel Lives." *Index on Censorship* 35, no. 2 (2006): 85-90.

Casanova, José. "Religion, the New Millennium, and Globalization." *Sociology of Religion* 62, no. 4 (2001): 415-41.

Charry, Ellen T. "Becoming Friends." *Journal of Ecumenical Studies* 50, no. 1 (2015): 117-22.

Christian, Siregar. "Pluralism and Religious Tolerance in Indonesia: An Ethical-Theological Review Based on Christian Faith Perspectives." *Humaniora* 7, no. 3 (2016): 349-58.

Clague, Julie. "Political Theology Ten Years after 9/11." *Political Theology* 12, no. 5 (2011): 645-59.

Cox, Brian, and Daniel Philpott. "Faith-Based Diplomacy: An Ancient Idea Newly Emergent." *Brandywine Review of Faith & International Affairs* 1, no. 2 (2003): 31-40.

Creswell, Michael H. "Wasted Words? The Limitations of U.S. Strategic Communication and Public Diplomacy." *Studies in Conflict & Terrorism* (2017): 1-29.

Dakake, Maria Massi. "A Good Word Is as a Good Tree: A Muslim Response to the Interfaith Challenges of Vatican II." *Modern Theology* 29, no. 4 (2013): 188-200.

Danan, Liora. "A Public Diplomacy Approach to International Religious Freedom." *Review of Faith & International Affairs* 10, no. 3 (2012): 59-66.

Danforth, John. "Mobilizing Religion against Terrorism." *Brown Journal of World Affairs* 24, no. 1 (2017): 77-85.

Dickens, W. T. "Frank Conversations: Promoting Peace among the Abrahamic Traditions through Interreligious Dialogue." 397-420: Wiley-Blackwell, 2006.

Diez, Thomas. "Diplomacy, Papacy, and the Transformation of International Society." *The Review of Faith & International Affairs* 15, no. 4 (2017): 31-38.

Douglas, Walter, and Jeanne Neal. *Engaging the Muslim World Public Diplomacy after 9/11 in the Arab Middle East, Afghanistan, and Pakistan*. Lanham: Center for Strategic & International Studies, 2013.

Dutta-Bergman, M. J. "U.S. Public Diplomacy in the Middle East: A Critical Cultural Approach." *Journal of Communication Inquiry* 30, no. 2 (2006): 102-24.

Eck, Diana. "Interfaith Dialogue in the New Religious America." *Review & Expositor* 114, no. 1 (2017): 25-33.

Fabrycky, David. "U.S. Public Diplomacy and Religion in the Muslim World." *The Review of Faith & International Affairs* 3, no. 2 (2005): 25-30.

Farr, Thomas F. "Diplomacy in an Age of Faith." *Foreign Affairs* 87, no. 2 (2008): 110-24.

Faucher, Charlotte. "Cultural Diplomacy and International Cultural Relations in Twentieth-Century Europe." *Contemporary European History* 25, no. 2 (2016): 373-85.

Fountain, Philip. "Mennonite Disaster Relief and the Interfaith Encounter in Aceh, Indonesia." *Asian Ethnology* 75, no. 1 (2016): 163-90.

Fridlund, Patrik. "Double Religious Belonging and Some Commonly Held Ideas About Dialogue and Conversion." *Mission Studies: Journal of the International Association for Mission Studies* 31, no. 2 (2014): 255-79.

Fulton, Brad, and Richard L. Wood. "Interfaith Community Organizing Emerging Theological and Organizational Challenges." *International Journal of Public Theology* 6, no. 4 (2012): 398-420.

Gerstbauer, Loramy. "Faith in Religion's Reconciling Power." *Brandywine Review of Faith & International Affairs* 2, no. 2 (2004): 50-53.

Hames, Harvey. "How Do Conflict Situations Affect Our Faith Communities and Our Interreligious Relationships?". *European Judaism* 37, no. 1 (2004): 68-75.

Haug, Kari Storstein. "Possibilities and Limitations of Interreligious Scripture Reading." *Mission Studies: Journal of the International Association for Mission Studies* 31, no. 2 (2014): 157-70.

Hefner, Robert W. "Christians, Conflict, and Citizenship in Muslim-Majority Indonesia." *Review of Faith & International Affairs* 15, no. 1 (2017): 91-101.

Hermansen, Marcia. "Muslims in the Performative Mode: A Reflection on Muslim-Christian Dialogue." *Muslim World* 94, no. 3 (2004): 387-96.

Hlaing Bwa, Saw. "Why Interfaith Dialogue Is Essential for Myanmar's Future." *Review of Faith & International Affairs* 13, no. 4 (2015): 71-78.

Holland, Claire, and Marney Walker. "Choice Theory and Interfaith Dialogue: Building Relationships between Faiths and Embracing Diversity." *International Journal of Choice Theory & Reality Therapy* 37, no. 2 (2018): 17-23.

Huda, Qamar-Ul. "Conflict Prevention and Peace-Building Efforts by American Muslim Organizations Following September 11." *Journal of Muslim Minority Affairs* 26, no. 2 (2006): 187-203.

Huff, Peter A. "The Challenge of Fundamentalism for Interreligious Dialogue." *Cross Currents* 50, no. 1/2 (2000): 94.

Hunt, Anne. "Interfaith Dialogue: Lessons from the Ecumenical Movement." *Compass* 44, no. 1 (2010): 8-13.

Irmgedruth, Rainer B. "The Religious Challenge: To Live in the Context of Diverse Cultures." *European Judaism* 37, no. 1 (2004): 54-59.

Jacobs-Vandegeer, Christiaan. "Navigating the Circle of Interreligious Dialogue and Theologies of Religions." *Australian e-Journal of Theology* 19, no. 3 (2012): 209-19.

Jafari, Sheherazade. "Local Religious Peacemakers: An Untapped Resource in U.S. Foreign Policy." *Journal of International Affairs* 61, no. 1 (2007): 111-30.

Javier, Edgar. "Interreligious Dialogue: Historical Constants and Challenges in Asia." *Philippiniana Sacra* 42, no. 125 (2007): 229-48.

J.E.W. "Interfaith Dialogue." *Journal of Church and State* 4, no. 1 (1962): 5-10.

Johanson, Todd. "Pluralistic Inclusivism and Christian-Muslim Dialogue: The Challenge of Moving Beyond Polite Discussion toward Reconciliation and Peace." *Journal of Ecumenical Studies* 51, no. 1 (2016): 31-53.

Johnston, D. "Faith-Based Diplomacy: Bridging the Religious Divide" Wheatly Papers on International Affairs https://wheatley.byu.edu/wp-content/uploads/2017/08/Douglas_Johnston_WebVersion.pdf. Accessed on: 21/1/2019.

Johnston, Douglas. "Introduction: Beyond Power Politics." Chap. 1 In *Religion, the Missing Dimension of Statecraft*, edited by Douglas Johnston and Cynthia Sampson, 3-8. New York: Oxford University Press, 1994.

Johnston, Douglas. "Looking Ahead: Toward a New Paradigm." Chap. 15 In *Religion, the Missing Dimension of Statecraft*, edited by Douglas Johnston and Cynthia Sampson, 316-38. New York: Oxford University Press, 1994.

Johnston, Douglas. "Review of the Findings." Chap. 11 In *Religion, the Missing Dimension of Statecraft*, edited by Douglas Johnston and Cynthia Sampson, 258-65. New York: Oxford University Press, 1994.

Johnston, Douglas M. "An Asymmetric Counter to the Asymmetric Threat." *American Foreign Policy Interests* 35, no. 1 (2013): 9-14.

Johnston, Douglas M. "Introduction: Real Politik Expanded." Chap. Introduction In *Faith-Based Diplomacy: Trumping Realpolitik*, edited by Douglas M. Johnston, 3-10. New York: Oxford University Press, 2003.

Johnston, Douglas M. "Religion and Foreign Policy." In *Forgiveness and Reconciliation: Religion, Public Policy and Conflict Transformation*, edited by Raymond G. Helmick and Rodney Peterson, L. Philadelphia: Templeton Foundation press, 2002.

Johnston, Douglas M. *Religion, Terror and Error: U.S. Foreign Policy and the Challenge of Spiritual Engagement*. California, United States: Praeger, 2011.

Johnston, Douglas M., and Brian Cox. "Faith-Based Diplomacy and Preventive Engagement." Chap. 2 In *Faith-Based Diplomacy: Trumping Realpolitik*, edited by Douglas M. Johnston, 11-29. New York: Oxford University Press, 2003.

Johnston, Douglas, Cynthia Sampson, Strategic Center for, and Studies International. *Religion, the Missing Dimension of Statecraft*. New York: Oxford University Press, 1994.

Jütte, Daniel. "Interfaith Encounters between Jews and Christians in the Early Modern Period and Beyond: Toward a Framework." *The American Historical Review* 118 (2013): 378-400.

Kanas, Agnieszka, Peer Scheepers, and Carl Sterkens. "Religious Identification and Interreligious Contact in Indonesia and the Philippines: Testing the Mediating Roles of Perceived Group Threat and Social Dominance Orientation and the Moderating Role of Context." *European Journal of Social Psychology* 46, no. 6 (2016): 700-15.

Kayaoglu, T. "Explaining Interfaith Dialogue in the Muslim World." *Politics and Religion* 8, no. 2 (2015): 236-62.

Khan, Humera. "Interfaith Contributions to a Just Society." *European Judaism* 48, no. 2 (2015): 46-53.

Khatib, L. "Public Diplomacy in the Middle East: Dynamics of Success and Failure." *Diplomatic Studies* 6 (2011): 133-47.

King, Roberta R. "Music, Peacebuilding, and Interfaith Dialogue: Transformative Bridges in Muslim–Christian Relations." *International Bulletin of Mission Research* 40, no. 3 (2016): 202-17.

Kovacs, Amanda. "Indonesia's Religious Conflicts: Recent Developments, Causes and Policy Implications for Peace". *The German Journal on Contemporary Asia* 127 (2013).

Kronish, Ron. "Interreligious Dialogue in the Service of Peace." *Cross Currents* 58, no. 2 (2008): 224-46.

Küng, Hans. *A Global Ethic for Global Politics and Economics*. Oxford University Press, 1997.

Lazenby, J. Mark. "On 'Spirituality,' 'Religion,' and 'Religions': A Concept Analysis." *Palliative and Supportive Care* 8, no. 4 (2010): 469-76.

Lebow, Richard Ned. "Constitutive Causality: Imagined Spaces and Political Practices." *Millennium – Journal of International Studies* 38, no. 2 (2009): 211-39.

Leggewie, Claus. "Dialogue? Thank You, No! Ten Commandments for Interfaith Dialogue." *European Judaism* 37, no. 1 (2004): 103-10.

Lowry, Carmen, and Stephen Littlejohn. "Dialogue and the Discourse of Peacebuilding in Maluku, Indonesia." *Conflict Resolution Quarterly* 23, no. 4 (2006): 409-26.

Luttwak, Edward "The Missing Dimension." Chap. 2 In *Religion, the Missing Dimension of Statecraft*, edited by Douglas Johnston and Cynthia Sampson, 8-19. New York: Oxford University Press, 1994.

Lynch, Cecelia. "Christian Ethics, Actors, and Diplomacy: Mediating Universalist Pretentions." *International Journal: Canada's Journal of Global Policy Analysis* 66, no. 3 (2011): 613-28.

Magonet, Jonathan. "The Growth of Interfaith Dialogue." *European Judaism* 48, no. 2 (2015): 38-45.

Mahmood, Tariq. "Interfaith Dialogue and British Muslim Prisoners." 586-603: University of Pennsylvania Press, 2016.

Mandour, Tayseir. "Islam and Religious Freedom: Role of Interfaith Dialogue in Promoting Global Peace." *Brigham Young University Law Review* 2010, no. 3 (2010): 885-93.

Mannion, Gerard. "Pathways for Dialogue in the 21st Century: What We Learned at Assisi 2012." 2013.

Marsden, Lee. "Faith-Based Diplomacy: Conservative Evangelicals and the United States Military." *Politics and Religion* 7, no. 3 (2014): 475-98.

Marshall, Paul. "The Ambiguities of Religious Freedom in Indonesia." *The Review of Faith & International Affairs* 16, no. 1 (2018): 85-96.

Mauro, Mario. "Religious Aspects of Politics." *European View* 11, no. 2 (2012): 157-61.

McCormack, Mark M. "Interfaith Relations in the United States: Toward a Multilevel Community Psychology Approach." *Journal of Community & Applied Social Psychology* 23, no. 3 (2013): 171-86.

McLarren, Katharina, and Bernhard Stahl. "'Hybrid Actors' – Religion and the Shift Towards a World Society" In *ECPR General Conference* Montreal 2015.

Mendes-Flohr, Paul R. "Reflections on the Promise and Limitations of Interfaith Dialogue." *European Judaism* 46, no. 1 (2013): 4-14.

Merdjanova, Ina. "Overhauling Interreligious Dialogue for Peacebuilding." *Occasional Papers on Religion in Eastern Europe* 36, no. 1 (2016): 26-33.

Merino, Stephen M. "Religious Diversity in a "Christian Nation": The Effects of Theological Exclusivity and Interreligious Contact on the Acceptance of Religious Diversity." *Journal for the Scientific Study of Religion* 49, no. 2 (2010): 231-46.

Miller, Kent D. "Interfaith Dialogue in a Secular Field." *Management Research Review* 40, no. 8 (2017): 824-44.

Ministry of Foreign Affairs, Republic of Indonesia "Bali Interfaith Dialogue" https://www.kemlu.go.id/en/berita/siaran-pers/Pages/Bali-Interfaith-Dialogue.aspx. Accessed on: 3/12/2018.

Mitwally Ibrahim, Mohammad Said. "Interfaith Dialogue a Muslim Legal Perspective on Its Validity, Concept and Practices." *Insights* 3, no. 1 (2010): 93-126.

Mor, Ben D. "Credibility Talk in Public Diplomacy." *Review of International Studies* 38, no. 2 (2012): 393-422.

Munjid, Achmad. "Building a Shared Home for Everyone – Interreligious Dialogue at the Grass Roots in Indonesia." *Journal of Ecumenical Studies* 43, no. 2 (2008): 109-19.

Munthe, Fredy. "Religious Movements in Humanitarian Issue: The Emergence of Faith-Based Organizations (Fbo) in Diplomacy Sphere." *Jurnal Hubangan Internasional* 5, no. 2 (2016): 172-80.

"Muslim Proposal Towards a Common Base of Interreligious Dialogue." *Advocatus* 14, no. 28 (2017): 1-14.

Muwahidah, Siti Sarah. "Interfaith Dialogue at the Grassroots Level: A Case Study of an Interfaith Empowerment Program in East Java, Indonesia." *Political Theology* 9, no. 1 (2008): 79-92.

Neufeldt, Reina C. "Interfaith Dialogue: Assessing Theories of Change." *Peace & Change* 36, no. 3 (2011): 344-72.

Nichols, Bruce "Religious Conciliation between the Sandinistas and the East Coast Indians of Nicaragua." Chap. 5 In *Religion, the Missing Dimension of Statecraft*, edited by Douglas Johnston and Cynthia Sampson, 64-87. New York: Oxford University Press, 1994.

Nickel, Gordon. "The Use of Sūra 3:64 in Interfaith Appeals: Dialogue or Da'wa?", 346-55: Paternoster Periodicals, 2016.

Nisbet, Erik C., and Teresa A. Myers. "Anti-American Sentiment as a Media Effect? Arab Media, Political Identity, and Public Opinion in the Middle East." *Communication Research* 38, no. 5 (2011): 684-709.

Obama, Barack "Remarks by the President on a New Beginning" https://obamawhitehouse.archives.gov/the-press-office/remarks-president-cairo-university-6-04-09. Accessed on: 4/12/2018.

Omar, A. Rashied. "Embracing the "Other" as an Extension of the Self: Muslim Reflections on the Epistle to the Hebrews 13:2." *Anglican Theological Review* 91, no. 3 (2009): 433-41.

Orsborn, Catherine. "Shoulder to Shoulder with American Muslims: What the Interreligious Community Is Doing to Combat Anti-Muslim Bigotry in America." *Journal of Ecumenical Studies* 51, no. 2 (Spring 2016 2016): 257-63.

Orton, Andrew. "Interfaith Dialogue: Seven Key Questions for Theory, Policy and Practice." *Religion, State & Society* 44, no. 4 (2016): 349-65.

Pallavicini, Yahya. "Interfaith Education: An Islamic Perspective." *International Review of Education / Internationale Zeitschrift für Erziehungswissenschaft* 62, no. 4 (2016): 423-37.

Parker, Lyn. "Religious Education for Peaceful Coexistence in Indonesia?". *South East Asia Research* 22, no. 4 (2014): 487-504.

Patel, Eboo. "Preparing Interfaith Leaders: Knowledge Base and Skill Set for Interfaith Leaders." *New Directions for Student Leadership* 2016, no. 152 (Winter 2016 2016): 75-86.

Pawlikowski, John T. "The State of the Global Catholic-Jewish Dialogue." *Studies in Christian-Jewish Relations* 5, no. 1 (2010): 1-4.

Pedersen, Lene. "Religious Pluralism in Indonesia." *The Asia Pacific Journal of Anthropology* 17, no. 5 (2016): 387-98.

Phillips, Andrew. *War, Religion and Empire: The Transformation of International Orders*. Cambridge: Cambridge University Press, 2011.

Philpott, Daniel. "The Challenge of September 11 to Secularism in International Relations." *World Politics* 55, no. 1 (2002): 66-95.

Philpott, Daniel. "The Religious Roots of Modern International Relations." *World Politics* 52, no. 2 (2000): 206-45.

Pohl, Florian. "On the Role of Interreligious Dialogue in Religious Studies Programs at Indonesian State Islamic Universities." *Journal of Ecumenical Studies* 50, no. 1 (2015): 159-66.

Pokhariyal, Ganesh Prasad. "The Influence of Religion, Technology, and Economy on Culture, Diplomacy, and Peace." *International Journal on World Peace* 32, no. 2 (2015): 41-50.

Pope Paul VI. "Declaration on the Relation of the Church to Non-Christian Religions: Nostra Aetate" http://www.vatican.va/archive/hist_councils/ii_vatican_council/documents/vat-ii_decl_19651028_nostra-aetate_en.html. Accessed on: 14/11/2018.

Portaankorva, Jari. "Muslim and Christian Leaders Working Together: Building Reconciliation in the Sierra Leone Conflict." *Journal of Pan African Studies* 8, no. 9 (2015): 79-97.

Pratt, Douglas. "Christian Discipleship and Interfaith Engagement." *Pacifica* 22, no. 3 (2009): 317-33.

Rieger, Joerg. "Occupy Religion: Theology of the Multitude and Interreligious Dialogue." *Buddhist-Christian Studies*, no. 34 (2014): 167-72.

Rugh, William A. *American Encounters with Arabs the "Soft Power" of U.S. Public Diplomacy in the Middle East.* Westport, Conn.: Praeger Security International, 2006.

Sakai, Minako. "Building a Partnership for Social Service Delivery in Indonesia: State and Faith-Based Organisations." *Australian Journal of Social Issues* 47, no. 3 (2012): 373-88.

Sandal, Nukhet A., and Patrick James. "Religion and International Relations Theory: Towards a Mutual Understanding." *European Journal of International Relations* 17, no. 1 (2011): 3-25.

Sapp, Christy Lohr. "Obama's Interfaith Service Challenge: A Call for a New Theology of Service in American Higher Education." *Dialog: A Journal of Theology* 50, no. 3 (2011): 280-88.

Seib, P. *Religion and Public Diplomacy.* Palgrave Macmillan US, 2013.

Seib, Philip. "Introduction." Chap. Introduction In *Religion and Public Diplomacy,* edited by Philip Seib, 1-7. New York: Palgrave Macmillan, 2013.

Seib, Philip. "Religious Freedom and Us Public Diplomacy." *Review of Faith & International Affairs* 11, no. 1 (2013): 15-21.

Sharp, Paul. "Crazy Religion Diplomacy." Chap. 12 In *Diplomatic Theory of International Relations,* 243-65. United Kingdom: Cambridge University Press, 2009.

Sheetz-Willard, Julia, Per Faaland, Rebecca Mays, and Angela Ilic. "Interreligious Dialogue Reconsidered: Learning from and Responding to Critique and Change." *Journal of Ecumenical Studies* 47, no. 2 (2012): 249-71.

Shoemaker, Terry, and James Edmonds. "The Limits of Interfaith? Interfaith Identities, Emerging Potentialities, and Exclusivity." *Culture and Religion* 17, no. 2 (2016): 200-12.

Smith, Huston. *The Illustrated World's Religions: A Guide to Our Wisdom Traditions.* San Francisco: Harper Collins, 1994.

Stack, Trevor, Naomi R. Goldenberg, Timothy Fitzgerald, and Brian Brock. *Religion as a Category of Governance and Sovereignty.* Leiden, Netherlands and Boston, Massachusetts: Brill, 2015.

Sunarko Ofm, Adrianus. "Interfaith Dialogue and Cooperation across Faiths: The Experience of Indonesia." *Theology Today* 73, no. 1 (2016): 46-59.

Suomala, Karla. "Complex Religious Identity in the Context of Interfaith Dialogue." *Cross Currents* 62, no. 3 (2012): 360-70.

Swidler, Leonard. "Deeper Meanings of Dialogue Today." *Journal of Ecumenical Studies* 48, no. 2 (2013): 143-44.

Swidler, Leonard. "Sorting out Meanings: "Religion," "Spiritual," "Interreligious," "Interfaith," Etc." *Journal of Ecumenical Studies* 49, no. 3 (2014): 373-83.

Takim, Liyakatali. "From Conversion to Conversation: Interfaith Dialogue Inpost 9-11 America." *Muslim World* 94, no. 3 (2004): 343-55.

Tan, Eugene K. B. "Faith, Freedom, and Us Foreign Policy: Avoiding the Proverbial Clash of Civilizations in East and Southeast Asia." *Review of Faith & International Affairs* 11, no. 1 (2013): 76-78.

Tebay, Neles. "'Papua, the Land of Peace': The Interfaith Vision and Commitment for West Papua." *Exchange* 36, no. 4 (2007): 337-58.

Thompson, Livingstone. "Religion and Diplomacy." *The Hague Journal of Diplomacy* 10, no. 2 (2015): 197-214.

Tiemeier, Tracy Sayuki. "Interreligious Reading in the Context of Dialogue: When Interreligious Reading 'Fails'." *Modern Theology* 29, no. 4 (2013): 138-53.

Todd, Nathan R., Jaclyn D. Houston-Kolnik, and Rachael L. Suffrin. "Understanding Community Issues of Interfaith Groups." *Journal of Community Psychology* 45, no. 2 (2017): 160-77.

Troy, Jodok. "Faith-Based Diplomacy under Examination." *The Hague Journal of Diplomacy* 3, no. 3 (2008): 209-31.

Tyagananda, Swami. "Doing Dialogue Interreligiously." *Dialog: A Journal of Theology* 50, no. 3 (2011): 227-30.

United States Institute of Peace. "What Works? Evaluating Interfaith Dialogue Programs ": United States Institute of Peace 2004.

"US and Cuba: Remaking of a Relationship." *Strategic Comments* 21, no. 3 (2015): 1-3.

Wendt, A. "On Constitution and Causation in International Relations." *Rev. Int. Stud.* 24 (1998): 101-17.

Zia-ul-Haq, Muhammad. "Muslims' Participation in Interfaith Dialogue: Challenges and Prospects." 613-46: University of Pennsylvania Press, 2014.

Zinnbauer, Brian J., Kenneth I. Pargament, Brenda Cole, Mark S. Rye, Eric M. Butter, Timothy G. Belavich, Kathleen M. Hipp, Allie B. Scott, and Jill L. Kadar. "Religion and Spirituality: Unfuzzying the Fuzzy." *Journal for the Scientific Study of Religion* 36, no. 4 (1997): 549-64.

Author Biography

Scott Blakemore, is a Ph.D. Candidate and Tutor in International Relations at Bond University. His research includes *Chinese Regionalism: China's Engagement with ASEAN and SCO* (Culture Mandala: Bulletin of the Centre for East-West Cultural and Economic Studies, 2014).